- To Dan -

Dream Big !

✦ **FROM KINGS PARK TO OMAHA** ✦

BOBBY HANEY

First Published 2011

Manufactured in the USA

ISBN-13: 978-1467946742
ISBN-10: 1467946745

Edited by Erika Watts • Cover Layouts by Craig M.
Cover Photography by Juan Blas/TheBigSpur.com
Back Cover Photography by Jeff Haney • Other Photo Credits:
Juan Blas/TheBigSpur.com • Richard Valeo, Huntington, New York
Gaines DuVall Sports Portraits • Andy Gregory • Lauren Romano
Alana Buckley • Danielle Ragosta • MaryEllen Gambardella
Brandon Haney • Bill Haney

From Bobby Haney:
This is the story of my life. The information in this book is true to the best of my knowledge. Many people, both in baseball and in the stands have assisted me on my journey...sorry if I have left anyone out.

I thank God for my abilities and for the people I have met in my life.

◆ DEDICATION ◆

I dedicate this book to my parents, MaryAnne and Jeff Haney.
None of this would be possible without my mother and father.
They are always there for me, no matter what happens in my life.
They made all the right decisions for me and still guide me
on the right path today. I thank you, Mom and Dad.

✦ IN MEMORIAM ✦

In loving memory of Donn Haber.
A wonderful family man,
a true sports fan,
and a great friend of the Haney family.

"One of the beautiful things about baseball is that every once in a while you come into a situation where you want to, and where you have to, reach down and prove something."

– Nolan Ryan, Hall of Fame Pitcher

"From the first time I saw Bobby run out to shortstop as an eighth grader, his body language screamed 'baseball player' to me. The way he carried himself and the passion and respect he had for the game showed every time he took the field."

> – *Denis Durland,*
> *Legendary Kings Park High School Coach*

"Bobby's passion for baseball went well with his fun loving personality. He was a perfect fit for our baseball program. Bobby was a great teammate and one of the best defensive shortstops in school history."

> – *Coach Tim Hill, Sr.,*
> *Greatest Baseball Coach in Junior College History*

"It was obvious that the physical gifts were there and above everyone else. He has solid gifts. He is a great person and has the makeup. He is an awesome leader and loves to compete. The thing that's best about Bobby is how humble he is. He is someone you enjoy being around."

> – *John Musmacker,*
> *Philosopher and Summer League Baseball Coach*

"The quick-witted Bobby Haney is also quick with his hands, arm and feet. The shortstop defense that Bobby played in our 2010 National Championship run will go down in history as one of the best in program history."

> – *Coach Ray Tanner,*
> *Head Coach, South Carolina Gamecocks*
> *Two-Time NCAA National Champion*

◆ FOREWARD ◆

Like all kids who play baseball, Bobby Haney had a dream, and that dream was to be part of a national championship winning team, and more importantly, to spend his life playing baseball. With the support of his family, friends and hometown, Bobby made it from high school to college, where he would become a part of college baseball history.

In 2010, all 290-plus division I college baseball teams knew that they had one last chance to make it to Omaha, Nebraska and play in historical Rosenblatt Stadium before the College World Series was moved to a new stadium, TD Ameritrade Park in Omaha. Only eight teams would go on to make it to Omaha, including the team Bobby played shortstop for, the South Carolina Gamecocks. Prior to 2010, the Gamecocks never managed to win a national title in any major sport, so not only did the 2010 baseball team have a chance to make CWS history, they had the opportunity to make school history as well.

The South Carolina Gamecocks take their nickname from Thomas Sumter, a notable figure and war hero in South Carolina history. Sumter was given the nickname for his fighting techniques and tendency to never back down. Bobby Haney and the 2010 South Carolina Gamecocks baseball team epitomized that nickname. When they found themselves with a loss in their first game in Omaha and one loss away from being sent home, they went on to win six straight games, securing their spot in college baseball history.

Today, Bobby is still playing the game he fell in love with as a kid, and is proof that with enough heart and determination, a childhood dream can be turned into reality.

By Erika Watts, Editor

⬧ CONTENTS ⬧

Chapter One - The Will To Keep Winning...13

Chapter Two - The KP Days...33

Chapter Three - Getting Competitive..45

Chapter Four - The Choices And Opportunities.........................57

Chapter Five - The Cloudy First Year In The Sunshine State.................71

Gallery...78

Chapter Six - You Never Know Who's Watching........................89

Chapter Seven - First Year As A Gamecock................................97

Chapter Eight - The National Championship.............................111

Chapter Nine - I'm Not In College Anymore.............................121

Epilogue...129

Why I Wrote This Book...131

Acknowledgements..132

◆ CHAPTER ONE ◆
The Will To Keep Winning

Planning a trip to the home of the College World Series in Omaha does not happen in the blink of an eye—it takes extremely hard work and leadership from the heart. As a team, we always felt it was possible to arrive at the famous Rosenblatt Stadium™ every year because we were the University of South Carolina Gamecocks and we could do anything. The Gamecocks always field a strong team, but there was something a little different about the 2010 season. We had our entire starting pitching staff back from the year before and most of our starting lineup. The most important thing that we had—which people don't often consider—was leadership. With eight returning seniors our organization had a chemistry unlike any other in the country. I knew that it was going to be a special year when I first stepped into Coach Ray Tanner's office before the season began. I said, "Coach, I think this could be the best team that I've ever been on." He agreed with me at the time, but was trying to stay as humble as possible—that was Coach Tanner for you. It was easy to talk, but we wondered if we could really live up to all the hype in 2010. There was only one way to find out. NCAA Division I Baseball starts out with nearly 300 teams from across the country. Of those teams, only eight make it to Omaha, Nebraska—that's right, eight teams.

The 2010 season started out with a bang; we swept Duquesne and felt good about ourselves. However, after that series came a little challenge: we had to travel to play East Carolina at their place in a three-game series. It was like crawling back into the lion's den after they walked off against us the year before to advance to the Super Regionals. We wanted revenge and we wanted it bad. Unfortunately, that revenge wasn't had, as we won our Friday game but lost the next two. That bus ride back to Columbia was a quiet one. When we got back to the stadium, Coach Tanner gave us ten minutes to get into the locker room for a meeting. This was not going to be a regular team meeting, either. Coach Tanner said, "Pitchers, pack up and go home—everyone who is a hitter, stay here." Coach Tanner explained to us how it was never acceptable to lose. Now, I know that no coach likes to lose, but Coach Tanner *really* did not like to lose—if you know what I mean—especially early in the season like this. He ripped on us so bad in that locker room that we didn't know what to do or think when he left, but one thing was clear—we knew that we had some serious work to do.

The next weekend didn't go as planned, either. We had a three-game series with our biggest rival, the Clemson Tigers. They're the team with the tight white pants and the orange and white cleats, and they have a coach who likes to dog pile into his team to jack them up before each game. Clearly, the South Carolina-Clemson rivalry is intense and is taken very seriously. The three-game series with the Tigers is held at three stadiums. One game is played on their turf at Doug Kingsmore Stadium, one game is played at our place at Carolina Stadium and the third game is held on a neutral field—that year we played at Fluor Field in Greenville, home of the Greenville Drive (class 'A' ball – Boston Red Sox).

We lost a heartbreaker to Clemson on the Friday night game at their place. We were still struggling with our bats and were not hitting the ball as we should have, with the exception of our catcher Kyle Enders, who was hot at the plate. On the next day, our game was at Fluor Field. Half of the fans in the stadium were wearing garnet and the other half were wearing bright orange shirts that I would only use to wash my car. The game was intense as we had about 10,000 fans and a great ballpark atmosphere. It was so loud in the stadium that our left-fielder Robert Beary didn't hear me calling for the ball on one play, which caused me to suffer a minor injury. I caught the ball, flipped over Beary and sprained my shoulder all in one play. We managed to get the win, 7-5, which felt like a load off of our backs.

The next day I was in a sling on the bench watching us try to grab the rubber game of the three-game series at our place in Cola, as most people refer to South Carolina's capital. The game started bad and snowballed from there. We ended up losing at home to Clemson and they took the series from us, their first series win since 2006. This was not just an ordinary loss, it was our worst loss at home in the two years since Carolina Stadium opened, and it was to our biggest rival. The score was 19-6 that afternoon. The Clemson Tigers stole our pride and owned us on our own field that day. I thought to myself, "You have got to be kidding me! How did we lose to a bunch of guys wearing orange and purple jerseys?" It was a major embarrassment to our school and to our beloved fans, which shows in part how intense the rivalry is. However, in baseball, no matter what happens you have to flush it and move on to the next game. From here on out we wanted revenge, and we would get it down the road.

We continued to battle through our long season and ended up beating the teams that we should have beaten. That Sunday loss to Clemson had a major impact on the rest of our season because from there on out we did not lose a midweek game. Even though the teams we play in midweek games are not that great, it is an impressive stat. It would have been easy to take the success of the rest of the regular season for granted and slack off, but we always played hard and played every game as if it was our last.

The one SEC weekend series that stood out in my mind was the Vanderbilt series. We showed the country how strong our pitching staff really was during that series. Blake Cooper got the win on Friday night, and even though Sam Dyson pitched his tail off on Saturday, we suffered a loss to the Commodores. Jay Brown then shut the door on Sunday and we took the series. To cap it all off, Coach Tanner got his 1,000th win as a college coach that game and it was breathtaking as we poured cold Gatorade® down his back. After that game, this team was back on track and more confident than ever. We beat Vanderbilt at their place in Nashville and won an important conference road series.

As we progressed through the rest of the regular season, we were neck and neck with the Florida Gators and stood together at the top of the SEC East. Sure enough, we were going to play at home against the Florida Gators in our final regular season series. The Gators had our number the year before, sweeping us clean at their place down in Gainesville, but this was our house. Whoever won the series would be crowned the winner of the SEC East and the winner of the SEC overall. Things didn't work out the way we imagined it. Florida took two of the three games from us and won the series. The worst part about that series to me was not that we lost the division, but it was the fact that after the Gators beat us in the second game on Saturday, they dog piled on our field in front of our home fans. That was so devastating to watch and made me furious inside. After the game was over, I went into the bathroom and smashed the paper towel dispenser, with my left hand, of course.

After the regular season ended, we still had a monster record of 43-13 and high hopes of doing well in the post-season, but before the postseason started, the SEC Tournament was first. Last year the team that won the SEC tourney, LSU, went on to win the College World Series. The trip to Birmingham for the tournament did not go well. It lasted about three days and was the shortest trip we had all year. Issues from earlier in the season came up again, and we just could not hit the baseball at all. We played two games and then we were sent home by the power slugging Auburn Tigers. LSU went on to take the SEC Championship once again.

On our bus ride back to Columbia that afternoon, Coach Tanner made it clear that nobody would be talking or laughing for the six-hour trip back home. He told us that since we were out of school, that when we got back to Columbia we would be starting two-a-day practices every day for the rest of the week until playoffs started. We looked at him and wondered, "Is this guy serious right now?" But, believe me, if you could see his face at that moment, you would know exactly how serious he was. When he was talking, Coach Tanner was speaking directly to the hitters on the team because the pitching staff kept us afloat all season. We did two-a-days, and it was no fun at all. We had to practice from 10:00 to 12:00, eat lunch, practice again from 2:00 to about 3:00 and lift weights afterwards. We were physically and mentally drained going into the Regionals.

Once the two-a-day practices came to a halt, the post-season arrived and we were psyched up. This Regional was special because it was the first Regional we hosted at Carolina Stadium. The Regional was double elimination—if your team lost twice, you were sent packing. Our hands were full with the teams in the Columbia Regional—Bucknell, The Citadel and Virginia Tech.

We had Bucknell in our first game and we still couldn't find a way to hit the ball again. We were losing early in the game by a couple of runs and still couldn't find a way to make anything happen. Luckily, the rain hit us hard and the game was delayed for about an hour and thirty minutes. During the rain delay in the locker room, some goofball on our team came up with a bizarre idea. We all shut the lights off in the locker room and gathered around in a circle. Like creatures in the wild, we made noises and we held on to each other. We figured that by now we would try anything to help make us a better ball club. After the rain delay was over, we came out red-hot and sprayed the ball all over the field. We were scoring runs, making plays and getting timely hits whenever we needed. We ended up beating Bucknell and shortly after that, the 'spirit stick' was born. The spirit stick was a metal fungo bat with garnet, gray and black tape around it. A baseball was also taped to the sweet spot on the barrel for added effect. We kept the spirit stick with us throughout the rest of the journey through the Regionals, Super Regionals and CWS.

The next team we faced was our semi-rivals, The Citadel, who was also from South Carolina. We had our fierce competitor and workhorse on the mound, Blake Cooper, and we were ready to go into battle. The Citadel started their number one pitcher, Asher Wojciechowski, who was a first round pick in the upcoming MLB Draft. He was blowing fastballs by us early in the game, with balls getting up to 93 and 95 MPH. Late in the game, I led off with a single up the middle, Scott Wingo laid down a perfect bunt base hit and we eventually took the lead. We ended up beating The Citadel in Game 2 and we were one win away from advancing to the Super Regionals.

In the next game in our Regional, we faced Virginia Tech, who was ranked in the Top 20 of the polls, just like us. The only problem Virginia Tech faced was that they had to beat us twice in order to advance to the Supers, which just wasn't going to happen on our turf. We knew going into the game that this was going to be a great matchup. We had the advantage throughout the whole Regional since we played in our stadium with our home crowd behind us. Early in the game, we were being shut down by their top pitcher and could not get any timely hits. As the game carried on and we got deep into Virginia Tech's bullpen, we started coming up with leadoff hits and big runs to put us on the board. After we had the lead for a while, we were wondering whether to dog pile after the game. When the last out was made and we beat Tech 10-2, everyone ran to the mound and hugged and shook hands, but did not dog pile—we decided to save that for an even better victory. We won three games in a row, won our regional and had a strong momentum going into the Super Regionals. It was just a small step we accomplished to get to Omaha, Nebraska. We were excited since this is what we had worked for all year.

After we had the regionals secured under our belts, we felt that we had more momentum than any other team in the country because our team would just never stop fighting, plus we had the 'spirit stick' by our side the whole time. The next day we had to sit and watch to see who we would play in the Super Regional. We were going to play the winner of the College of Charleston-Coastal Carolina game. If Charleston won, we were going to play them at our home field in Columbia, and if Coastal won, we would play Coastal at their place in Myrtle Beach. We were hoping we would play Charleston so that we would have the home field advantage again. Coastal ended up beating Charleston, so we were headed to the beach. We were excited, but we knew that we had work to do and there was no time to mess around—as Coach Tanner always says, a road series is considered a 'business trip.'

When we first got to Coastal it was just as hot as it was in Columbia, and maybe even hotter. Everyone enjoyed the strong ocean breeze, but it felt more humid and much hotter on the field. After we arrived at the hotel, we had practice a few hours later. When we arrived at the field, Coastal had just finished practicing. As they were walking through the gate off the field, we were walking through the gate to the field. We made eye contact with each and every one of them to let them know that this wasn't their house anymore.

After we finished stretching and getting loose, we noticed Coach Tanner standing in centerfield by himself. Coach Tanner called the whole team over to where he was standing and told us all to turn around and face the infield. Coach Tanner said, "Marzilli, you're a smart guy, turn around to the infield and tell me, what do you see?" Marzilli replied, "Um, a batting cage, stadium seats and home plate." *(It was clear that he was wondering where Coach Tanner was going with this, as we all were).* Coach Tanner said, "Everyone look at the pitcher's mound and imagine yourselves dog piling in the middle of that infield." That got us pumped up and we knew we had to give it our best and make that happen. After he said that, we all went nuts and then took the field for practice.

At practice, we went through our normal routines of hitting and fielding and goofing off, like us Gamecocks do best. We were dropping bombs in batting practice because Coastal had short fences down either line, especially down the leftfield line, which was only 310 feet. It was so hot in practice I almost felt like I was going to pass out and everyone was giving me crap for it. I'm a New York boy; I can't handle the heat like the southern boys can. After a good practice, we packed it up and headed back to the hotel to get ready for game 1 the next day.

The next morning we were pumped to play the Coastal Carolina Chanticleers in game 1 of the Super Regionals. Nerves were running high before the game, and the stands were loaded with just as many Gamecock fans as Chanticleer fans. Scott Wingo did his ritual speech in front of the dugout and told us that he 'Googled' a Chanticleer. Wingo said, "A Chanticleer is a baby Gamecock, so they are already calling us their daddies!" Wingo was great at motivating us. It was one of his best speeches yet, and he had us all fired up.

We were the away team wearing Yankee grays and Coastal was the home team in white. We jumped right out of the gate with a 3-run lead in the first inning starting with the rising young freshman, Evan Marzilli. We later scored in the early innings again to make the lead 4 to nothing. We were confident in our lead with Blake Cooper on the mound, but that short porch in leftfield was in the back of our minds. Sure enough, in the second inning Coastal hit a line shot into the leftfield seats to creep within 2 runs. Later on in the fourth inning, Coastal put a couple of base hits together and scratched another run across the board to bring them within 1. We knew now with the hot weather and the short porch in leftfield that it was anybody's ball game. In the fifth inning, Coastal loaded the bases with one out against Coop and were threatening to take their first lead of the game. Cooper gave up a hotshot ground ball up the middle; Coop stuck his glove out and deflected the ball up the middle toward the shortstop side. As I was about to take charge and turn two, Wingo came out of nowhere, grabbed the ball, fell on the bag, and turned the double play unassisted. I stood there in disbelief of what had just happened. It was Scott Wingo to the rescue!

After that, the momentum was totally in our favor and we secured the one run lead in the later innings. In the eighth, we were once again in a bases loaded situation, and this time, there were no outs. It was then time for our closer Matt Price to get to work. When Matty came in, the team had all the confidence in the world in him, and so did he. He struck out the first two batters and then got a ground ball comebacker to him that he quickly shoveled off to first base. Matty did his classic fist pump and we escaped danger again going into the ninth inning. Believe it or not, later on in the bottom of the ninth, Coastal had runners on first and second, with two outs, and were threatening again. The next batter hit a moon shot to center to our All American, Jackie Bradley Jr. Jackie caught the ball with ease. The game was over and game 1 of the Super Regionals was ours!

If you think that game 2 was going to be laid back, you are sadly mistaken. Game 2 of the Super Regionals was one of the most nerve racking baseball games that I have ever been a part of. In game 2, we had our flamethrower and top round pick in Sam Dyson on the mound, and we had a good chance of making our way to Omaha. Unfortunately, this game did not turn out as planned. It was an absolute slugfest between both teams, but we weren't going to let the Chanticleers stand in our path.

In the first inning, Dyson gave up a solo shot and the momentum swung back into the hands of Coastal with their home fans right behind them. Not to worry; we answered back in the bottom half of the inning with a string of hits resulting in two runs. The next inning Dyson was a little rattled and gave up 3 runs. Dyson had a short outing, giving up four runs on four hits in two innings, and Jose Mata came in to clean up his mess. Mata gave up a run before he got out of the inning, resulting in us being down 5 to 2. In the third inning, Coastal made two errors, which we capitalized on by Adam Matthews hitting a huge 2-run double to bring us within 1 run. Coastal tacked on a couple of more runs and we fought right back with a couple of clutch hits of our own. It was knotted up at 7 runs a piece going into the seventh inning, and then our restless bullpen that had been the best in the country all year gave up two runs to make the score 9 to 7, Coastal. Our bullpen was toast and we pretty much used everyone except for the stallion Matt Price. Down by 2 going into the bottom of the eighth, we knew that we needed to at least tie the game, or else we were in a bad spot. We had a leadoff guy on, and then Whit Merrifield, one of the best hitters in the history of Carolina baseball, hit into a double play.

After that, we needed some garnet and black magic to happen fast. Jackie Bradley Jr. then drew a walk to get on and Adrian "Clutch" Morales hit a double down the line to put runners on second and third, with two outs. That brought our freshman phenom, Christian Walker, to the plate. Walker was not getting anything to hit at all, just slider after slider, down and out of the strike zone. Walker was down in the count 1-2, and we needed a miracle to keep us from playing the next day. The next pitch was a slider that didn't slide; it backed right up into Christian Walker's barrel and landed back in Columbia! I couldn't believe it; Christian Walker hit a 3-run homer to put us up by one going into the ninth inning.

After the third out was made, the momentum was clearly on our side. When we took the field, I looked to the bullpen and sure enough, making his way to shut it down was Matt Price. I was pumped to get these last three outs. It felt as though there was an hour between each out that was made. Matty got the first guy to strike out and the second guy to fly out to right. The South Carolina Gamecocks were now one out away from going to Omaha, the final destination. Price dealt and a high chopping ground ball was hit right at me. I thought to myself, "Oh my God, this is it, we are going to Omaha." I fielded it cleanly then threw it low to Walker at first; he came up with the grab and our gloves hit the sky. We put Coach Tanner's dog pile picture into reality, with me being stuck on the bottom of the pile on Coastal's home turf. One of the greatest feelings I ever had in my baseball career was being at the bottom of that pile!

After we all climbed out of the dog pile, I started to hug every one of my teammates with a huge smile on my face. Everywhere I looked someone was smiling from cheek to cheek and hugging each another. It was as if God sent us the greatest gift in the world, and we were truly the best. One person I will never forget hugging was Coach Ray Tanner. I said, "Congrats Coach!" and he picked me up off the ground and screamed, "You almost bounced it! You almost bounced it!" as he was shaking me up and down. I didn't know how to react, except to laugh. It was one of the happiest days of both our lives.

After we got back to the hotel from winning, we all went down to the beach as a team and did a dead sprint into the ocean for a victory swim. All of the people on the beach were staring at us wondering what we were going to do next. We didn't care about anything at that point; we were on top of the world and nothing was going to bother us now. We were one of the eight teams in the country to make it to Omaha out of the 64 teams that made it to the playoffs.

The next thing the fans and our parents had to do, which we talked about from day one, was book our flights to Omaha, Nebraska. I was so pumped that we were going because we worked so hard for it, and everything has to go your way in order for you to go. We were a great ball club with a little bit of luck on our side, as well. Sometimes it's better to be lucky than good.

When we arrived back in Columbia after the Super Regionals, there was all kinds of talk about us on the radio, especially about Christian Walker who was the savior for our team with his go ahead 3-run homer. The radio stations talked about how big the home run was, and how Walker will be one of the most honored Gamecock players in the history of Carolina baseball. The radio was even talking about the girl at the game with me and wondering if it was my sister or my girlfriend—it was my girlfriend, Danielle. Danielle and I were in the car listening to the radio at that time and got a kick out of that. It was so great to feel the support of the fans and the great atmosphere we were surrounded by back in Columbia. It still was not over yet as we had a trip to plan and a lot of work to do; the next stop was Omaha!

I don't think that any of us on the team really cared about how great we did in Omaha; we were just so excited to be going there. We had our own sendoff at Carolina Stadium with a crowd of about a thousand adults and little kids. There were ten-year-old little leaguers that lined the hallways giving us all high fives as we departed to the airport. Coach Tanner then gave a speech to our great fans and we were off!

The plane ride was nothing special, just a bunch of us idiot baseball players playing card games for fun. When we arrived at our hotel in Omaha, we were greeted by everyone from the Embassy Suites hotel—the managers, the secretaries, the maids, you name it. They were all out there to meet us and make us feel at home. We were located in a great area in Omaha, near where all the fans stay, with great bars and restaurants. When you're in Omaha during the time of the College World Series, it is the biggest event going on in the country. Almost everyone knew who you were and knew what team you played for, and if they didn't, they would ask you anyway.

Before the tournament started, we had a nice barbeque with all of the College World Series teams, followed up with a ceremony on the field. The last eight teams standing were South Carolina, Clemson, Texas Christian, UCLA, Florida, Florida State, Arizona State and Oklahoma. The opening ceremonies for the beginning of the World Series were breathtaking. All eight teams were introduced one by one from centerfield in front of a packed house of about 25,000 fans. At the ceremony, the College World Series 'Legend Team' was introduced to the crowd with stars such as Nomar

Garciapara, Robin Ventura, Barry Bonds, Will Clark and many others who shined throughout their college careers. All the teams and coaches had their cameras out and their eyes wide open like little kids in a candy store. The legends gave speeches about their playing days and how great of an experience the College World Series is. To finish off the ceremony, Rosenblatt held a half-hour fireworks show over the bleachers, along with a video on the JumboTron. The video showed all the greatest memories and highlights that took place over the years in Rosenblatt Stadium. This was the last CWS that would take place in Rosenblatt, and we knew back in February that we had to make it to Omaha to play there and become a part of history.

Two days later, the South Carolina Gamecocks took on the Oklahoma Sooners for our first game of the CWS. Every year when the World Series is played in Omaha, the weather forecast is gorgeous, but that was not the case when we played the Sooners in game 1. The weather was awful, with rain and lightning filling the air every other hour. The weather was so bad that the start of the game was delayed a little over four hours. The Sooners had the lead the entire game, while we were sluggish at the plate with our bats. We didn't want to lose our first game in the College World Series because we would then be one loss away from packing our bags and going back to South Carolina. The lightning picked up so bad that the game was delayed again for another two hours in the middle of the sixth inning. We then went back into the locker room, only down by one run, as the rain started to hit Rosenblatt hard. It felt like we spent all day in the locker room and dugout. We left the hotel at 11:00 in the morning and it was approaching 8:00 at night. After the rain let up a little, we took the field and gave up another run in the eighth, giving the Sooners a 4-2 lead. In the ninth, we battled back, getting a run, and then we had the bases loaded with Gamecocks and our clutch hitter at the plate. Adrian Morales had worked his magic all postseason, but he popped up to centerfield on the first pitch he saw and we were 0-1 in the CWS.

At this point in time, we weren't enjoying our stay in Omaha. It poured, with our first game being delayed by more than six hours, and we didn't get back to the hotel until about 11:00 at night. Something had to change, and change fast, or else we were headed back to Columbia.

The next day was an off day and we needed it more than anyone, especially after the day we had before. Two days after the rain and lightning were over, we were struggling to stay alive in the loser's bracket. Joining us in the elimination game was the top ranked team in the country, Arizona State University. There was no room for error. We had to win this game, and in order to do that, we had to come out aggressive. After struggling with the bats in game 1 against the Sooners, our bats woke up with Merrifield, Morales, Walker and the Cocks steamrolling Arizona State by a score of 11 to 4. We were still alive and still very hungry as we were getting a little closer to the National Championship Series.

After getting a much needed win under our belts, the next day we did what many college teams do when they are in Omaha. We decided to visit the Children's Hospital & Medical Center in Omaha that day. When we walked into the hospital, we just had a good feeling and were happy to be there to visit the children. Some of the children were suffering from cancer, while others suffered from diabetes and other diseases. When we walked in, the faces of the children and their parents lit up the room. We spoke to some of the kids and asked them their names. We signed a baseball for almost every kid in the hospital that day. When we got to one room, the mother told us that her little girl loved watching baseball with her father.

She said that her daughter loved to watch baseball and got lost in the game. When I placed the autographed baseball in the little girl's tiny hands, her eyes were so wide I couldn't believe it. Her mother was right; she was just drawn to the game of baseball. When we were talking to one of the nurses, she said that every year the team that visits the Children's Hospital goes on to win the College World Series. We didn't think anything of it because we thought that every team visited with the kids.

The next day was finally here, and we were once again playing the Oklahoma Sooners. This game was considered life or death because it was an elimination game for the both of us. There was once again no real offense in this game from either side, but the pitching was stellar from Blake Cooper. The score was tied at one a piece going into extra innings, and no one could find a way to score a run. We entered the top of the twelfth inning and the catcher for Oklahoma hit an opposite field home run off of our stud relief pitcher, Ethan Carter. The Sooners knew that this game was over, and the chances to advance were in their favor. Carter was devastated, and the wind was taken right out of us. We had to go into the bottom of the 12th with a positive outlook, no matter what happened.

Robert Beary, who played once every three games, got on base with a single and ended up at second with two outs to keep our hopes alive. We were now down to our last out in Omaha with the tying run on second base. Coming to the plate was our best hitter in Jackie Bradley Jr. Jackie worked the 'at bat' better than anyone. Jackie had two strikes on him, and we were now down to our last strike of the season. The next pitch to Jackie was right on the inside corner. The umpire yelled, "Ball!" The next pitch was thrown, Jackie swung and drilled it sharply through the hole past the first baseman, bringing Beary in to score the tying run! We were back and it was a whole new ball game. Jeffery Jones then drew a walk to put Jackie on second base. Our most feared hitter of the season, Brady Thomas, stepped in the box with Jackie as the winning run on second. The first pitch Brady saw, he swung and hit a seed up the middle, which brought Bradley in for the score! The Gamecocks were still alive in Omaha. Jackie and Brady were later interviewed by the gorgeous Erin Andrews from ESPN.® We were now a serious contender in Omaha.

It didn't get any easier for us in Omaha because now we had to face our biggest rivals dressed in orange, the Clemson Tigers, who had our number from earlier in the year. As we were one game from elimination, we had to beat Clemson not once, but twice in order to reach the National Championship Series. Their bats were hot and to get a win against them was not going to be an easy task. We had to be focused, but at the same time, stay as loose as possible.

Cooper and Dyson were not ready to pitch yet because they had to rest, so the pitching decision was up in the air. Right before we got off the bus at Rosenblatt, a couple of guys said that Michael Roth was starting, and it was true. Our lefty specialist out of the bullpen was getting the start against Clemson in the CWS. We thought it was a good move considering 7 out of the 9 hitters in Clemson's lineup batted lefty.

We started off strong and hit the ball around the yard and executed better as a team, putting up 5 runs in the first six innings. Roth, on the other hand, was dominant giving up only 1 run and pitched a complete game against the boys in orange. It was the gutsiest pitching performance I have ever seen and a great decision by the coaching staff. We were now one win away from going to the Championship Series against the pretty boys from UCLA.

When we faced Clemson again, it was an elimination

game for both of us, so you knew it was going to be a good game. The winner of the game would have the chance to go on to make history for the state of South Carolina. We had our fire baller on the mound in Sam Dyson, and he gave us a solid performance once again. We beat Clemson 4-3 and advanced to the Finals with back-to-back victories over them. Even though losing the series against Clemson earlier in the season had stung, what sweet revenge it was to be the team that knocked them out of Omaha.

We were now one series away from bringing home a national championship for the University of South Carolina or going home empty handed. This was what all young baseball players dream about—taking home a championship. My love for the game started as a young kid in New York, and now I was only two or three games away from taking home a national championship with my team.

◆ CHAPTER TWO ◆
The KP Days

My hometown is Kings Park, Long Island, New York, which is part of the township of Smithtown. I considered myself a normal kid growing up in a normal family, and like most kids I had tremendous dreams. I dreamt of being a major league ballplayer. Kings Park is what someone would call a small town and is home to around 17,000 people. It is the kind of town where everyone knows their friend's business and what was going on with each other. At anytime somebody can go into a store or a deli and always find someone in there that they know, whether it is someone from church, a friend, a teacher or a former baseball coach. The people are great and the pizza and bagel places are second to none. After all – this is New York! Kings Park is a good town for sports, particularly baseball, softball and football. There is no college sports atmosphere in Kings Park like in some other towns in the country so sports fans root for high school sports and move right on to the Yankees and Mets. The fans in Kings Park are very supportive of their teams - at home and away games. Wherever I end up in life – Kings Park will always be special to me.

My earliest memory of playing baseball is when I would hit Wiffle® balls in the backyard of my grandparents house in Commack, NY, with Great Grandma Tootsie pitching to me when I was two. My mother and father claim that I started to swing a baseball bat soon after I started walking, and at 1 months old I was swinging and hitting balls from anybody that would pitch to me. Then again, my Mom and Dad both argue that I was named after the famous Bobby Murcer of the New York Yankees, but actually, I was named after both of my Grandfathers, Robert and William. Growing up I loved a lot of sports, but the only ones that I truly enjoyed playing were baseball and basketball. I started playing at age 4 in the St. Joseph's Catholic Youth League. My dad was my baseball coach, just like he was for my older brother Brian, and both my mom and dad ran CYO basketball for many years. As I got a little older, I played a lot of baseball with my friend Chris Hoffman, and his dad, Bob, coached us for years and taught us the basics. Baseball was everything to us.

The summer that I was seven going on eight was a highly memorable one, but almost terribly tragic. I always rode my bike up and down the vast hill in front of my house, because I thought it was so cool to go fast just like every other kid I knew. One morning I went out riding by myself. I came flying down the hill in front of my house and up my driveway. As I came up my driveway, I hit the front lip so hard and fast that I flew off my bike into a small tree. The side of my face hit a branch, and blood poured out everywhere on my driveway. My little brother Brandon was about four at the time and didn't know what to do or how to react. As the blood dripped from my face, I walked up to the front porch, crying. My mom and dad, along with my older brother, Brian, came running out of the house and were shocked to see that the left side of my face was a mess. My dad did not even have a shirt on when he put me in the car along with mom and took off for the hospital. On the way I kept asking my mom "Is it bad? Is it bad?" She told me it wasn't, but I knew it was awful. At the hospital, my mother was still holding the rag over my face to keep the blood from dripping on the hospital floor. We had to wait all afternoon for the plastic surgeon to get to the hospital and when he arrived he did a great job – over 50 stitches! To this day, I have an extremely long scar across the left side of my chin—it looks sexy now, but it didn't at the time. I still wonder what would have happened if my parents were not home, or what if the branch went through my eye or throat. I thank God every day that things worked out OK for me. I was glad to have my family and relatives with me, and a great doctor to fix me up. Everyone really took care of me!

After that dramatic part in my life, I considered giving the bicycle a rest for a little while and focused on sports. Around ages 9 and 10, I started to play in a league known as KPY or Kings Park Youth. I also played in a travel league with my friends in the summer called the Kings Park Vipers and the Kings Park Kingsmen. KPY was highly competitive because games were played during the school year and not in the summer. The great thing about KPY was that there was a 'draft' for all the teams, so the teams would be even. All my friends were scattered out on different teams each year and we were considered rivals once the games started. The teams were named after Major League teams, so some of us played for the Mets, Yankees or Marlins. My team was the Rockies my first year and the Orioles the year after that. I played both shortstop and pitcher at the time, but was mainly the closer in games that came down to the wire. I used to throw gas when I pitched at 45 feet. In both of those first 2 years we won the championship with Bob Wilborg as my coach, and my dad as the assistant. From there on out, winning was in my blood and losing was just not acceptable.

I loved playing basketball almost as much as baseball. I was a fairly fast point guard and could dribble the ball as good as anyone, but was not the best shooter. I played a lot of basketball at the time, but I was more driven to play baseball. My best friends also played basketball, and that was part of the reason why I played for so long. I had minor knee problems and problems with my feet because I was growing so fast, and I thought it was from the basketball court, so I decided to play baseball exclusively when I was 12. Unfortunately, this decision didn't stop the problems with my feet. After baseball games, I would barely be able to walk because the pain was so miserable. My coach at the time, John Dekams, was very upset for me because he knew there was a problem and he knew I loved the game. I couldn't walk anymore and my season came to an end. My arches were hurting me all of the time, and it felt like a bruise when someone would touch it. We all knew that this was not normal and something needed to be done.

After months of pain and no relief from custom insoles (orthodics) in my shoes, my mother and father on a recommendation from my pediatrician decided to take me to the best pediatric orthopedic doctor in New York, Harold Van Bosse. To our amazement, and within 2 minutes of being examined, the doc said I had an accessory navicular in both feet. This is an extra small bone that I was born with and is found in the arch area. The extra bone was not in a good position and it was causing me to be in severe pain. There was only one way to solve the problem. The doctor came right out and told us that I would need surgery to fix my feet. The doctor said that he would have to go in and shave the bone down on each arch in order to decrease the amount of pain I was experiencing. When the doctor recommended surgery, I was devastated and looked to both of my parents for help. My mother and father agreed with the doctor 100 percent, which made me very upset. I thought to myself that surely there had to be another way around this. I didn't want to go through surgery because I was scared, and in my young mind, I didn't think that I would ever be the same again. Everyone agreed that the quickest way for me to get back to walking without pain and playing sports again was to operate on both feet at the same time. The worst thing about it was that I would have to spend the summer wearing casts on my legs and I would need a wheelchair to get around. Bummer!

The day before surgery, I tried not to think about it, but I was so upset and could not help but cry at the time. Sure enough, at 6:00 in the morning, I was in surgery and had both legs wrapped up with casts up to my knees. When I woke up from surgery and saw the casts, I felt like I was in another world. I was released from the hospital a few days later and my father drove as slowly as he could all the way home from the city to our house so I wouldn't get jerked around and be in any discomfort.

When I got home, I realized that I was going to spend my first summer as a teenager in casts up to my knees with nothing to do. This was extremely difficult for a teenage boy who was as active as I was. Every night for two weeks, I had to sleep with my legs elevated to make sure the swelling stayed down. I couldn't take a shower, so I would have to wash myself with a washcloth or a towel all the time. I felt like the biggest loser on the planet. Every one of my friends was outside all the time enjoying summer and playing baseball. Meanwhile, I was laid up inside my house with giant casts on my legs. Some of my friends did come over the house to see how I was doing and signed my casts, and people in my neighborhood would also come by to cheer me up.

Seven weeks after I had the surgery was the week I was waiting for. This was the week that I was finally going to get the casts taken off my feet. There was only one problem—my doctor was not available that week because he was out of town on vacation. I was extremely upset and furious because I wanted the casts off my feet as soon as possible. Into the eighth week, my doctor was finally available and ready to remove the casts. He had a mini electric saw that softly cut through the casts. It didn't hurt one bit. I was so excited when I saw my legs and feet and couldn't wait to start walking again. I got up off the table, stood up, and I almost fell down. It felt so awkward, like I was standing on uneven ground or something. I thought I would be able to walk right out of the casts, but that wasn't the case at all. I could barely even stand up straight.

The doctor gave me a walker to use around the house for support. That made me even more upset, because I felt like I was 90 years old! It was so embarrassing, and now I was worried that I might never walk again. My mom was so upset she started to cry and was asking my dad, "Why can't Bobby walk?" My mom called the doctor at his office a bunch of times asking what the problem was. The doctor said it was normal to be unable to walk right out of the casts and that it would take some time to build up my muscles and get used to walking again. A couple of weeks later, I started to walk again and was feeling great. The surgery was a success and I was out of the woods at last. To this day my father still says he is saving the casts for the Hall of Fame in Cooperstown, NY!

After I decided to focus only on playing baseball, my parents bought me whatever they thought would help me to improve. One summer they bought me what we called a 'PitchBack™.' A PitchBack is a device that rebounds the baseball to you after you throw it into the tight netting. My Dad had built a basketball court in the backyard, but since I didn't use it for basketball, I would use it for the PitchBack fielding surface. In the corner of the court, there was another device called a SwingAway® that my parents also bought me. The SwingAway batting station had a baseball tied to three strings and was connected to a plate. You could hit all day without having to fetch a baseball, unlike the tee where you would need to replace the ball every time. The ball would go right back to its place between the strings, and you could re-adjust the pitch. If major league players were using it to get better, I wanted it too.

One of the greatest things about the basketball court was that my father built lights over it, so at nighttime I was all set. My little brother Brandon and I would sometimes be outside until 1:00 in the morning and would throw balls off the Pitch-

Back to each other. My father's rule about hitting off the SwingAway at night was strict. He made me hit with a wood bat at nighttime because the metal bat was too loud at night and could wake the neighbors. Everyday I tried to take 500 swings and field a few hundred ground balls. My buddy, who lives two blocks away from me would come up to me in school and ask, "Bob were you hitting for, like, three hours yesterday?" I told him that was me—I loved to play the game more than anyone did. People would always tell me that there are kids all over the world practicing just as hard as I was, but I thought that there was no one in the world who could possibly love the game of baseball more than me.

I wasn't a big fan of Halloween growing up. One Halloween I decided to stay home and not go trick or treating with my friends. What 14-year-old boy does not like to trick or treat on Halloween, right? That Halloween I was outside throwing the baseball against my PitchBack for hours, while people walked up my street looking at me as if I were crazy. I didn't care what other people thought about me or what they said to their parents and friends. I just loved the game.

Winters living in New York were devastating for me because it was so cold and I could not go outside to practice. Some winters I would actually take the SwingAway inside my house and swing downstairs in my basement. Sometimes, just to keep my arm in shape, I would throw a baseball straight into my futon, so there would be no noise and nothing would get broken. When that got boring, my little brother Brandon and I would then play our own game of baseball in the basement. There were no runners or bases, but there were outs and strike-outs. We would get a bunch of loose-leaf paper, roll it up into a tight ball and tape it up with clear tape. It was childish, but it was a good time. Each side was given 2 outs and we played until we struck out twice, and then we would change sides.

We would play the game for so long that we would lose track of time and forget about everything else. The only problem with playing baseball in the basement was that my father's workspace was down there. He called the room "His Area." We usually stopped when my dad came down to work because we always made too much noise.

Every day down in the basement there would be either a new scratch or a new dent in the wall or on one of my dad's Mickey Mantle pictures. One time my brother threw me an inside pitch and I smashed it off of my father's Winslow Homer painting. The photo was about three feet by five feet hanging on the wall and was covered by a pane of heavy glass. I hit the paper ball so hard that the painting fell off the wall and plummeted straight to the ground. I could feel my heart almost skipping beats as the painting fell to the ground. The painting hit the floor and the glass pane shattered. Brandon and I both looked at each other and started to laugh at first, and then the possibility of getting in trouble dawned upon us. Thankfully, no one was home at the time, so we quickly picked up every piece of glass and hid it so no one would ever find it. My brother and I then hung the painting back on the wall without the glass as if nothing had ever happened. My parents never noticed it and my brother and I escaped that punishment. To this day, the painting still hangs downstairs without the glass.

Whenever I practiced the game of baseball, whether it was during the winter or summer, rain or snow, inside or outside, I knew that I had to practice the right way. There is a phrase people always say, "Practice makes perfect," but that is not exactly the case. The correct saying should be, "Perfect practice makes perfect." You have to learn and understand at an early age that you have to practice and practice hard. My mother and father always told me, "Bobby, you have to practice hard because there are other kids in the world doing the same thing that you're doing right now." I didn't believe it at the time, but my parents were right and I had to listen to them. Like some of my other friends, we thought it would be a good idea to start taking hitting lessons at the Sal Agostinelli Baseball Academy that was nearby. It was one of the best things we ever did. My hitting instructor, Coach Chandler, worked with me once a week, and I do mean worked. After one of our lessons was over, he would be covered in sweat and would be exhausted. He taught me everything he knew about hitting and the right way to approach the baseball. Each week coach and I would work on a different technique and a different way to attack the baseball. He would always tell me to go home and work on it, and that's exactly what I did. would go in front of mirrors in my house and draw lines on the carpet with tape to make sure my feet were in the right position. During the next hitting lesson, I was ready to make the next jump. It was a huge learning step and helped me get to where I am today.

When someone loves something and never stops talking about that one thing they love, people say that you're obsessed. That's how I felt about the game of baseball. I was truly obsessed with the game and could never get enough of it. My heart belonged to the game, and I felt like the only reason I was put on the face of the earth was to play baseball, and that was it. My parents accepted the fact that all I wanted to do was play baseball. They were proud of me for working so hard and becoming a more polished baseball player every day. One night I went into my dad's study when he came home from work and I told him that I wanted to make it to the Major Leagues one day. He said, "You're going to get your shot one day, kiddo." Every single kid in the world loves to hear positive feedback from their father, I certainly did.

I took that positive energy from my dad and used it for

motivation everyday I played baseball. My mom and dad were the most supportive people in the world when I was playing travel baseball, and so was my entire family. That is what you need when you are chasing a dream like mine. If my mother and father did not take me to every travel game, my relatives would jump in and help – whether it was in New Jersey or upstate New York. After the games, they would treat me to the dinners that most kids consider the best—hamburgers! When you're young and you have a tremendous support group, it truly motivates you and makes you happy. I could never have done anything without the support of my parents and family. When my mother and I would get home from a two-hour drive from the city after a game, she would tell me to take off my uniform as soon as I got into the house. She would take my muddy pants and smelly shirt, go downstairs right away and throw it in the washer. This was just one of the ways my mom showed her support for me. She always made sure that my equipment was ready.

Every time I saw a kid around my age playing baseball or warming up before a game, I would always compare him to myself right off the bat. I would look at a team, find their best player that everyone talked about, and compare the two of us. I didn't care what other people said about him or me; I just knew inside that I was better, or going to be better than that kid.

People will probably not believe this if I told them, a big part of the reason for why I stopped playing basketball was because I knew that I wasn't the best player on the court. I never had fun at something that I was not the best at because I was a highly competitive little kid. Another main reason, of course, was that I just loved the game of baseball so much more. When I took the field as a little leaguer and as a baseball player, I thought to myself that I was easily the best player on the field. It was nothing for me to become cocky or arrogant over, but that's what I thought all the time. Even in the early teenage years and before that, I knew I had to be the best baseball player no matter what. I worked so much harder than so many other kids did, and there was no reason why I should expect myself to be anything but the best player on the diamond.

My father knew that there were times when I was going to fail and times when things were just not going to go my way. However, through it all, my father wanted me to change and make an adjustment for the best. My father would always say that he was proud of me, but he never said that I was the best or felt as if he had to sugarcoat anything for me. Dad always used to tell my mom that he wanted me on a team where I was going to be the worst player. I truly hated when he said that because I always wanted to be the best. The reason why he wanted me on a team where I was the worst player was so that I would be motivated to learn and get better as a baseball player. He wanted me to elevate my game to the next level. The most memorable quote from my father back then that he still uses today was "Step it up." Those three words meant a lot to me. It meant that I was not doing enough and it let me know that I had to put in more work. If I wanted to achieve my goals, I would have to go out and not only work hard, but outwork the other kids as well. My father was right when he said all those things, because not only was he making me a better player, he was making me be a better person as well.

No matter how far I get into my baseball career, I know I'll always look back fondly at my days growing up in Kings Park. From t-ball to high school ball, KP is where I developed my passion and love for the game. I hope that many other young baseball players in KP will decide to follow their dreams and one day make it to the college or pro level.

◆ CHAPTER THREE ◆

Getting Competitive

Someone who motivated me to stay competitive as a kid through high school was my idol, Derek Jeter. Not only did I want to try to be better than kids on the baseball field, I also wanted to try and push myself to be as good as he was. As many people know, Derek Jeter is the shortstop for the New York Yankees. Every girl on Long Island had a crush on him and every young boy wanted to be him. He played for my favorite team, so I never missed one of his games. I used to write down on a sheet of paper how many hits he had after every single game and add them all up after the end of the season. I tried to do everything like Jeter—hit like him, field like him, walk like him and even wear my hat the way he did. Some people *still* make fun of me for how I wear my hat. If he made a play while I was away from the television, I would get so mad. He was my idol and a true inspiration to many young children and baseball players around the world.

Every time I had the opportunity to go to a Yankee game with my friends or family, there would only be one player I would care about, and that was Derek Jeter. Usually I wouldn't even care about how the Yankees did, as long as he had a decent game. I know this sounds ridiculous, but when I was about 10 years old, I would actually compare myself to him and I thought I was just as good as he was. If he got two hits in a game and I only had one hit in my game, I would be mad that he did better than I did that day. I kept that part of baseball to myself and did not want anyone to know at the time. I watched Jeter so much on television that when I went to the games, I would think that I knew him, like we were best friends. When I stood by the edge of the fence right next to Jeter, I would hear other people shouting and screaming his name, but not me. I would just stand there, take it all in, watch the way he carried himself, and watch the way he warmed up before the game.

Whenever people ask me how I manage to pick up ground balls so gracefully and make it look so easy, I tell them that I practice all the time and I always try to emulate my favorite player, Derek Jeter. In the backyard, I would always throw the ball against my PitchBack and catch it exactly as he would in the game. In a game, when I would field a ground ball, I would always catch the ball and then do a shuffle before I threw it to first base because that was the way that he did it. I was never truly taught how to pick up a ground ball and throw it because no one really played baseball in my family. I learned from watching the man himself. I didn't know any other way to field a ground ball or throw a ball. It had to look like Derek, and if it didn't, I corrected it so it would. I used to love when parents and kids called me Jeter and told me that I looked like him when I played. That made me feel so calm and confident about my game. Sometimes the opposing team would call me Jeter and laugh about how I did everything like him.

My dad and mom also loved Derek Jeter almost as much as I did at the time because he was a winner and he played for the New York Yankees. The main reason why so many people loved him was because he never did anything wrong on or off the field. He always knew how to handle pressure wherever he was. Sometimes, some things came out in the paper about Jeter partying too much in New York City, but that was about all you heard as far as negative publicity went. You never heard anything about him getting arrested or taking steroids, as many major league baseball players do. He is a national and worldwide icon. He has a powerful image and always protects it extremely well. My mom and dad used to say, "Bobby, do you see how Derek never curses or gets mad when he gets out or strikes out?" They were right about him. He never showed any emotion when he got out or even made an error on the field. That was the extraordinary thing about him because many players show emotion after they make mistakes. Even in interviews after a game, he would never slip up and say anything unpleasant about his team or other people. He kept it "Vanilla," as Coach Ray Tanner of the Gamecocks would always say. Jeter kept his interviews very low key and almost colorless.

Derek Jeter would always talk about one thing and one thing only—winning. At the end of the day, it truly does not matter how well you performed or how well your teammates did, it only mattered whether you won the game. With Jeter playing for the most successful franchise in the history of sports, losing was not an option whatsoever. The Yankees were always a winning machine, and it has to remain that way forever. I loved Derek Jeter so much growing up that my favorite book was the one he wrote, *The Life You Imagine*. It was about how he grew up as a black boy in Kalamazoo, Michigan, where no one was ever going to make it big. In the book, he talked about how he was always made fun of by kids at school and in the neighborhood. The kids would call him names because his mother was white and his father was African American. It wasn't easy for him growing up as a kid, but he handled it better than anyone. His parents raised him the right way and taught him everything they knew, just like my parents did. After reading his book, I wanted to do everything he did, and be exactly like him growing up.

Even though I played shortstop like Derek Jeter, I was a lot different from him in a particular way because I was not a right-handed hitter. He is a right-handed hitter, and I was a left-handed hitter. I was kind of mad when I saw him bat because I knew that we didn't bat the same, but everything happens for a reason. My dad said that he didn't really teach me to bat left-handed; he said that I just picked up the bat one day and started to swing it from the left side, but that was weird because I threw and did everything else with my right hand. On the other hand, my little brother Brandon is the complete opposite since he hits right-handed and throws lefty. Brian, my older brother is like me – right-handed and swings lefty.

I just figured I was unusual that way because there are not many left-handed hitting shortstops. It's kind of odd and unique to find a left-handed hitting shortstop. I loved being different all the time and standing out, so batting lefty made me even more of a stand out to some people.

I always wanted someday to be as good as Derek Jeter, and in order to do that, I had to work constantly and stay competitive. Some days I would stay out on my basketball court taking swings and fielding ground balls until my parents went to bed. I knew that I couldn't slack off – ever, because I knew that Jeter always worked harder than everyone else did. When I read his book, he expressed how hard he worked to reach his biggest goal, and that was to play for the New York Yankees. He had such a different life than I had growing up. As for *my* family, we never had to deal with 'race' and being made fun of as much as Jeter's family did. When I think of that I am even more driven, because with all the hardships that he dealt with growing up, he shows that it is truly possible for anyone to accomplish their goals if they work hard enough.

Another way I stayed competitive as a kid was by playing travel baseball. Even though some kids are pressured into playing travel ball by other kids or their parents, I played because I knew that's what I wanted to do when I got older. My mom would sometimes ask me if I could ever stop loving the game of baseball because sometimes it does happen to some people. Some people just lose interest and get tired of it after playing the game for so many years. I always told my

mom that I would never stop loving baseball or playing t
game. I am still playing the game today and I still love it mc
than anything in the world.

When I reached the 7th grade, it was time for the "b
time"—the middle school baseball team. It was finally he
and at last, I was going to play for a school team instead of ju
a travel team, which increased the competition level. At th
time, my goal was to play shortstop for my middle scho
team, which I accomplished. I played shortstop and batt
over .450 in seventh and eighth grade.

After I dominated in middle school, I was a little cocki
but in a good way. I was confident in my own mind and d
not want anyone to know about it except me. I had the feeli
that if I was good enough, I could possibly make the varsi
baseball team as a high school freshman. This would be a hu
accomplishment for me in my career. My high school coac
Denis Durland, (also known as Duke), made the decision
put me on varsity. Coach was scary and intimidating, but
was the boss at the time. Throughout tryouts, I couldn't t
whether I was going to be on the junior varsity or the varsi
team. On the final day of tryouts, the two assistant coach
and Duke brought me into Duke's office and said, "Bobby, v
are going to go ahead and bring you up to varsity this year."
was shocked at the time and did not know how to act. Du
saw something in me and later said, "From the first time
saw Bobby run out to shortstop as an eighth grader, his bo
language screamed 'baseball player' to me. The way he carri
himself, the passion and respect he had for the game show
every time he took the field."

After I left the coach's office, I waited for my dad to pi
me up outside the school. I could not wait to see my dad ar
tell him the news. When dad picked me up, he was talking
another player's dad in the parking lot and I didn't want

say anything until we were alone. When my dad and I pulled away, he asked me how I did. I said, "Dad, guess what?" He said, "What?" I said, "I made varsity!" He could not believe it. We were so happy to celebrate the exciting news with all of our friends and family. I thought to myself, "Wow, I did it, I actually did it." I felt like I had accomplished the best feat in the world, and I didn't realize how much more work I had ahead of me. That was a terrific day and I will always remember it as the serious start of my baseball career.

During my freshman year of high school, I felt like the big man on campus wearing a varsity jersey while my friends wore their junior varsity jerseys. I thought I was cool riding around with my buddy Charlie Loparo, who was a junior on varsity at the time. As exciting as it was, I felt a little left out that I wasn't part of junior varsity since that's where my best friends were. I was able to get over that quickly, though, since varsity was waiting for me and I was loving the attention.

There was only one problem playing shortstop at the varsity level. A stud senior was already at that position. His name was John Dekams, and he also was the teams best player, plus he was my best friend's older brother. Fortunately, I didn't have to sit on the bench and try to beat out Dekams or wait for him to graduate. Since our team was hurting at third base at the time, John slid over to third while I played shortstop. Since it wasn't an issue for John to change positions, that made me think that John was looking out for me.

I performed okay my freshman year, but not as good as I wanted too. Handling the pressure at the varsity level was a big change from middle school. The competition was stellar and the game speed was much quicker. Despite the pressure, I batted just under .330 and made All-League as a freshman. The most remarkable thing about my freshman year was that we went undefeated in 18 league games. I could not believe it; my first year on varsity and we were undefeated. I was living the dream at the time. After we were eliminated in the second round of the playoffs, my freshman year came to an end. My coaches and I had extremely high hopes for my sophomore year.

One reason that I was always motivated to play ball in KP was because of the framed jersey hanging in our gym. There were some days I could not believe that I was going to the same high school that Craig Biggio went to. All I could think of was seeing my jersey hanging alongside his some day. I remember stories from some of the teachers and coaches about Craig – how he was a better football player than baseball player. But – look how it turned out – he had a great career with Houston, and he has a great shot to be going to the Hall of Fame – from Kings Park!

During the summer of my freshman year, I played baseball for a team called the Long Island Tigers. It was a travel team that played teams all over Long Island. This was one of the best summer teams I was ever a part of. My teammates were an exceptional group of guys to hang out with, and they were great baseball players as well. The reason why this team was so good was because of the coach we had, Lou Petrucci. Lou was one of the nicest guys you could ever meet, and an outstanding coach. What made Lou such a great coach was that he had an intense love for the game. Outside of the game, he was the nicest and most laid-back guy in the world. Lou knew more about the game of baseball than anyone I've ever met because he was a coach and an umpire and still is today. Lou is so passionate about what he has to say, and when Lou speaks, people don't just listen, they pay attention and remember the way he speaks about things. Lou would always put you before he put himself, that's just the way he was. That summer we played so strong that we made it all the way to the

FABL World Series in Oklahoma. In the final game of the World Series, we fell short and lost 20-17 to an Orange County team from California. It was a devastating loss, but was still an extremely fun trip with guys I loved.

When my sophomore year came around, my confidence level was higher than ever since I had a year of varsity baseball under my belt and had developed a more intense work ethic. One area of my game I needed to improve was the endurance and strength parts of my game, so, my dad signed me up for a gym that specialized in working with athletes. The gym was called Xcelleration™ and was structured to work on speed, endurance and strength. A man named John Furia on Long Island owned the gym, and many athletes soon started working out there. Standing no taller than 5 feet 6 inches tall, John Furia was the best trainer you could find in New York. John knew his stuff better than most trainers and even some doctors. If you needed to improve, then you knew to go to John. If you needed to get stronger, then go to John. If you had an injury, you would go to John. The man would dedicate his life to you in the weight room and help you get to the next level. By the end of the winter, more than half of the high school team was going to Xcelleration and seeing great results.

Each year that I played, my work ethic changed dramatically for the better because I was learning more and seeing results. I knew in order for me to succeed, I needed to continue improving. The most valuable thing about baseball and life is that you have to learn new things and make adjustments, day in and day out. Early in my teen years, I knew that I was not as fast as I used to be in middle school, so I had to do something about it. After each high school game, I would run sprints around the warning track a few times and try to condition myself and make myself a little bit faster. I thought it helped me become a better baseball player and get me into better shape. While I ran after a game, all of the other kids on my team would pack up their stuff and head home. As they walked to the parking lot, they would see me out there running around the warning track.

As a shortstop, I also have to maintain quickness and range up the middle and in the hole. I also did agility drills to improve. I would set up cones around my yard in about a 50-foot radius, would run and shuffle from side to side and back peddle as well. It helped me get quicker in short distances and it also made me more confident as an infielder.

Another major aspect that I had to work on to stay competitive was arm strength. Everyone knows that you cannot play shortstop unless you have a strong arm to reach from deep in the hole. I will be honest—I do not have the strongest arm in the world, but I could get the ball over to first base in a hurry. I weighed no more than 150 pounds throughout my teen years, so I needed all the arm strength I could get. I strengthened my arm by long tossing a few times a week and by using elastic bands. A main part of the equipment I used to strengthen my arm is the rice bucket. A rice bucket is strictly used for strengthening your whole arm, starting at the fingertips. I did this drill by dumping a couple of pounds of rice in a bucket, I then would stick my hand in up to my forearm in the rice and would work the muscles for about 20 minutes. I went from front to back, side to side, did figure eights and squeezed the rice for a 'grip' drill. The rice bucket is excellent for strengthening all joints and important muscles in the entire arm.

Some of my best friends were called up to varsity during my sophomore year, so I was happy about that. As a team, we struggled a little bit, went 11-7 and were knocked out early in the playoffs. Whenever you lose in the postseason, it's a massive letdown, especially with the teams we had growing up in KP. I had a much better year and hit in the upper .300s and received All League and All County honors. Kings Park High School was dedicated in baseball every year, and that always gave us a solid chance to win State. If a team won the State Championship, they would receive a championship ring. With the team we had coming back for my junior year, our confidence level and goals were through the roof. The team and I expected to win a championship.

All of my boys were back and were better than ever for our junior year in high school. We were all finally on varsity together: Reggie Smith, Nick Wiwczar, Ted Dekams, Dennis Murphy, Adam Melanson, Tom Locrotondo, Rob Brown, Mike Pearse, Rob Goldstein, Rocco Laudadio, Rob Aguece, Luke Mangogna, Chris Ripp, Joey Miron, and myself. We grew up playing baseball together since we were 10 years old and lived and died by Kings Park baseball. With the exception of a couple of players, we didn't play any other sport for the school except baseball. Baseball was in our blood, and we loved it. Junior year was a crucial year for all of us because it usually determined where we might be going to school in a couple of years, and college scouts were on the lookout. Once again, we had another exceptional year, but fell short in the playoffs during the game before the county championship.

Senior year finally came around, and as seniors, we felt cocky and we felt like we owned the school. The only thing I truly cared about my senior year was winning the state championship with my best friends. I could feel it—this was the year. At the end of the regular season, we went 18-0 again, just like our team from when I was a freshman. We had high hopes going into the playoffs, and nothing could stop us. In the first round we had to play out of our division against a heavily favored Commack team led by my travel-ball friend, Mike Belfiore. We surprised everyone by beating them on their own turf. The entire Kings Park team played well that day and it was a great victory for us. Next, it came down to KP playing East Islip in a do-or-die 1 game series. The winner would win the Suffolk County Championship and then move on to the Long Island Championship.

Though we were down 7-0 early in the game, we battled to tie the game in the final inning with our stud pitcher and my best friend on the mound, Reggie Smith. This kid had the biggest heart on the field and wore it on his sleeve. East Islip just kept finding a way to come up with key hits and made critical plays. They looked like a championship team that day as they won 8-7 and dog piled on their home field, sending us home. I was upset because I was a senior captain on my team, and my family and relatives were there watching every second of the game. High school baseball was everything to me and my friends. We were all devastated with the way our season ended. My high school career was officially over, and it ended with a loss. I knew I had to put that in the past and move on to the next chapter in my young baseball career.

◆ CHAPTER FOUR ◆

The Choices and Opportunities

⟩ be selected in the *Major League Draft*
...ng kid wanted to be picked because it
...า order for someone to become selected
to be a promising young baseball player,
bit of luck on your side. Every year there
is a di.... ...ared to other professional sports, the baseball draft is a little different. There are 50 rounds in the MLB
draft, whereas other sports such as football have less than 10
rounds. The reason why there are so many rounds in baseball
is because they need hundreds of new players each year to fill
spots in 30 MLB organizations around the country.

Some people think that when you are drafted in baseball
that you go straight to the big leagues, but that couldn't be
further from the truth. When you are drafted, you are sent to
the bottom of the barrel in the minor leagues, and you are no
longer a superstar. There are about five minor league teams
in every organization, and that's why the draft consists of so
many rounds each year. There are around 1500 players that
get drafted to the minor leagues each year, and only three to
five percent of those players make it to the big leagues. It is
still a serious honor to be selected by a major league team, no
matter what.

When I say 1500 kids are drafted each year in the MLB
draft, you may think that it isn't that tough to get selected, but
that is not the case at all. Professional scouts overlook even
some of the best players in the country every year. When you
are looking for 1500 players, you're looking at all of the
division I schools, division II schools, high schools, NAIA
schools and all junior colleges. You are also competing against
kids from Canada and U.S. territories, such as Puerto Rico.
You are competing with so many kids from 17 years of age to
about 22 years of age. You can't forget the kids who have
connections or had a father or relative that played in the major

leagues before, so those kids have it easier than anyone else. Sometimes kids are not very good at baseball and have poor attitudes, but they are still picked up because it's always about who you know. The baseball world is an extremely political world and it's not fair sometimes for players.

Some players who go to big division I schools put up terrible numbers, but they are drafted high because they went to a big DI. Players are sometimes drafted based only on their body type—tall, lengthy and skinny, with outstanding potential. Some kids get drafted just because they can run fast, but can't hit or field worth a lick. Sometimes I would look at a player and wonder how on earth he got drafted.

During my senior year, I was being recruited by a bunch of schools, but not the ones I had hoped for. I always wanted to go to school in the south or out west because I wanted to play baseball where it was warm all year round since I hated playing in the cold weather of NY. In the beginning of spring, during my senior year, there was only a little bit of talk about getting looked at by professional scouts for the MLB draft. I didn't think too much of it because I knew that I was going to college unless I got offered a lot of money in the draft.

Throughout my junior and senior years I received a couple of letters from big league teams. I was excited and honored. The letters are long questionnaires that you have to fill out, and that takes about 20 to 30 minutes. Scouts need to know all kinds of information on the person they are considering drafting, such as where he is going to school and key injuries throughout his career. I was just 16 years old when I started filling out the questionnaires, and I wanted to be drafted more than anything in the world. I didn't care about the team or how much money I would be offered. I thought it would be so awesome to be selected to the major league baseball draft. All little boys have dreams growing up that one day they will be chosen by a major league ball club, and I truly had a good shot of being selected. My name was very popular throughout the Long Island baseball community, and during my senior year, my chances of being drafted increased.

Every year the MLB draft usually takes place in the beginning of June. In 2006, our baseball season ended around May and I graduated at the end of June. A couple of days before the 2006 draft, my mom got a phone call from one of the area scouts in town. His name was Sal Agostinelli, and he was a scout for the Philadelphia Phillies. He told my mom that I needed to be in Philadelphia the next day, which was two days before the draft, for a pre-draft workout. When my mother told me the news, I was thrilled to go to the workout, but I didn't want to get too excited and get my hopes up. Going to this workout does not mean that you are going to be drafted, but it does mean that you have a very good shot at being drafted. My dad and I drove to Philly the next day. The stadium known as Citizens Bank Park was gorgeous. I was blown away by it. I didn't get the chance to perform too much due to bad weather, but I had a decent showing. We were limited to an inside workout under the stands. I was extremely nervous at the workout because there were successful college players there, and I was only a 145 pound 17-year-old at the time. After the workout was over, my dad and I said goodbye to Sal. He told us he would be in touch, but when scouts say things like that, you don't quite know what's going to happen. It was an honor to have been invited.

The night right before the draft I went online and searched through different websites to see if anything about the draft came up. I found one website that had a lot of information about the upcoming draft. The website was called MLB Draft Tracker, and it had a list of all players that were draft potentials. I searched for the letter 'H' in the last name column, and sure enough, I saw "Haney, Robert" listed. I was so excited and told my dad right away. He was also excited to see my name there, but we didn't truly know what it meant. Once again, we didn't want to get our hopes up and think that I was going to get drafted because I was on a draft tracker list. On the next day, the 2006 MLB Amateur Draft finally arrived. I was so excited because I knew some guys that had the potential to get drafted and I was also excited to see if my name would be called. Players selected in rounds 1 through 25 are usually announced on the first day of the draft, and rounds 26 through 50 are announced the next day. On the first day of the draft, I was in school and every chance I had to get out of class, I would go to the library and check the computer to see if my name or anyone else I knew got called. It was so exciting because I knew I had a decent shot of being picked. When the first day of the draft ended, I was a little upset, but not really surprised. I knew that I wasn't going to be selected that high even if I did get picked.

On the second day, the draft started a little later on in the afternoon because they picked players a lot faster through these rounds than the day before. I got home from school when they were a couple of rounds into the draft when my buddy Ted Dekams, brother of John Dekams, called me and invited me to the Yankee game that night.

The draft continued and when round 35 came up, I walked away from my computer and thought, "Oh well, maybe I'll get drafted another year." I was not even that upset since I was going to the Yankee game that night. When I walked away from my computer, I went upstairs and changed to go to the game. After I changed, I was on my way back downstairs when my friend Mike Pearse called my phone and asked, "Are you watching the draft?" I said, "Yeah, kind of, why?" He said, "You were just drafted!" I hung up on him and sprinted down my stairs. I checked the computer and sure enough, I read:

Philadelphia Phillies, 38th Round, 1147th pick of the draft, Haney, Robert, Shortstop, Throws R, Bats L

I could not believe my eyes. I can't explain the feeling. It was the best feeling in the world. I felt like my dream had finally come true that day downstairs in my basement. I then slowly crept upstairs and told my little brother Brandon the news. We hugged it out for about five seconds before I started making phone calls. The first person I called was my father. I called him up and said, "Dad, guess what?" He said, "Hold on one minute Bobby, I'm on the phone with a client." I couldn't believe my father put me on hold right when I was going to tell him I was drafted. I called my mom next. She was so thrilled and asked me if I had called dad yet. I told my mom that he put me on hold, so she told me to keep calling him. When I reached my dad again, I told him that I got drafted to the Phillies, and he said, "No you didn't!" He couldn't believe it either. He was so happy for me that he was crying in the middle of his office by himself. He knew how hard I worked for this day, and knew that I deserved it. A few minutes later, my scout, Sal, called me up and said congratulations on being selected by the Phillies. I barely said anything because I was so shocked and excited.

Soon after that, calls and text messages were blowing up my phone as if I had been elected president. Almost everyone I knew was texting or calling me and leaving voicemails. I was enjoying every minute of it, who wouldn't? I heard from all of my best friends, my little league coaches and my neighbors. I then headed to my friend's house so we could go to the Yankee game and all of his brother's friends were there congratulating me on the draft. It rained so hard that day that the game ended up being postponed. I was so bummed about the game being cancelled, but my parents were happy because they wanted me to enjoy the night with them. The Yankee game being rained out actually worked in our favor. When my parents got home, I shared massive hugs and kisses with them and they told me that this is the next step. My grandma and grandpa came over to the house a little later and they also shared the night with me—I loved everything and everyone at the time and felt like a million bucks.

Later on that night, the boys and I went to the mall to buy Phillies baseball hats. It felt so amazing that I could wear the baseball hat for the professional major league baseball club that drafted me. We walked into a baseball cap store in the mall and looked for the Phillies logo. We couldn't find a cap in my size, so we asked the people who worked there and one of my best friends, Nick Wiwczar told them that I had been drafted by the Phillies. The clerk didn't believe Nick at first, but then as we kept on talking about it, he believed us and he congratulated me. After finding the right sizes, we wore our hats out to dinner. When I got into the car to head to the restaurant, my buddy Dave Sommo told me that he bought me a present earlier in the day. He ordered me an authentic Phillies jersey with my name and high school number on the back of it. I thought that was awesome and it felt great to know that everyone was as proud of me as I was of myself. At one point during dinner, I went to the bathroom, and when I came back the entire restaurant was applauding and cheering for me.

My accomplishments throughout my life and my high school career did not even come close to the day that I was drafted. I have so many baseball memories throughout my young career, but nothing compares to that day. The greatest thing about getting drafted was sharing the day with my best friends and family in New York. You are nothing without your support group, and I had a fantastic one. One of the main reasons I am still playing baseball is because of all the love and support from all the people back home. My friends and their families are always watching me and following me throughout my career. That day I got drafted to the Phillies, I was easily the happiest kid in the world, but it also made my town proud as well. The 38th round of the 2006 MLB Draft and the 1147th pick overall is my round and my pick, and that is something no one can ever take away from me. I can always tell my kid and my grandkids that I was once selected in the MLB draft out of high school.

Just because I had hopes for being selected in the draft didn't mean that I would skip college and go straight to the pros. Unless you are drafted in one of the earlier rounds, you don't get much money, so I knew I would have to play some college ball to improve my draft status. I always wanted to go away to college because I knew that there was no way I could stay up north where the weather was bitter half the year. In New York where I lived, it was too cold to play baseball for more than six months out of the year, which is what helped make my college decision. I handled the cold weather fine throughout my high school and travel ball days, but I knew couldn't continue on with it. When I was little, I always talked about how much I hated the cold weather and how much loved the heat. I had to bear with the cold weather all through high school because I had no choice, but with college, I had choice of where I could play. It was a serious decision around my sophomore year of high school when my parents and talked about going 'away' to college. It didn't bother me that I was possibly going far from home, on my own, and my parents wanted what was going to be the best for me and my care

Even though I was a talented baseball player coming ou of high school, that didn't mean that I could get into any college I wanted. I told my dad that I wanted to play college baseball somewhere that was warm, such as Florida, Texas, or even California. Things didn't go the way I planned, though. During my junior year of high school, I was heavily recruited from schools in the north. I had interest from UConn, Kentucky, Indiana, Penn State, Old Dominion, Stony Brook, St. Johns and many other northern schools. These schools were great, but they were all located in a cold weather climate, and I couldn't go through with that anymore. I was good enough to play at schools in the south, but they never recruited me. It is hard to get recruited by large division I programs in the south when you live all the way up in Long Island, New York. I knew that if I was going to attend a school in the south that I would have to do all of the recruiting by myself.

When my senior year was approaching, my dad and I had to get to work fast. I was getting terribly nervous and almost scared when senior year was approaching, because I didn't have a clue where I was going to college. I kept thinking of what it would be like not going to college or not even getting a chance to play baseball ever again. I knew that my dad and I would work our hardest to get into the best baseball school possible, no matter what.

My dad is a very outgoing person and was never afraid to approach scouts or coaches or ask them questions about getting to the next level. During my travels with the L.I. Tigers, we had some great opportunities to be 'seen' because the Tigers were one of the best and most respected Travel teams on Long Island at the time. Don and Sue Whiston, who ran the organization, were excellent leaders and always put the players first. They ran a top notch organization and knew all

its, so naturally the scouts came to many L.I.
to see the talent. At one particular Saturday dou-
bleneader, our friend Gil Matos (I played with his sons Justin
Echevarria and Gil Matos) pointed out that Pat Short was at
the game. Pat was the Area Scout for MLB and lived on Long
Island. My dad, of course, met Pat, who was evaluating some
of the players at the game and found out that he hosted a
showcase for MLB scouts in the nearby county. Pat liked the
way I played, so I was excited to hear that I got an invitation
to the workout. It was one of my first showcase events and I
got a chance to perform – running, fielding and batting. It was
great. I performed pretty well and got a chance to see the
scouts and all the players in action. At the end of the event and
on the way to the parking lot my dad ran into another scout,
Neil Somers, who was retired, but loved to watch the kids play.
After speaking to Neil for a bit, (he has always given us great
advice) he said that if I wanted to get seen by the pros and
possibly play in the south I should try to get to the best showcase in the country, the East Coast Pro Showcase in NC. Well,
I did make my way to that showcase and I performed OK, and
there were 200 scouts and colleges. It was a great experience
and I met a lot of baseball people. I had to leave the showcase
a day early and fly directly from NC to Jackson, MS, to meet
up with my Tiger's team that was playing in the FABL
World Series.

My coach that summer and in Jackson, MS, was John
Musmacker, a brilliant coach, but a finer person than he is a
coach. We called him Coach Moosh for short. I had never
been to Mississippi in my life, but I liked playing there. When
I played in tournaments, I would always look around in the
stands to see if college scouts and pro scouts were there
watching, but sometimes you can't tell. You always have to
play hard no matter what, because you never know who is

watching. In the tournament, I played shortstop a٦
of balls hard with the wood bat. The competition was stellar,
as we faced guys who were committed to schools such as
Tulane, Ole Miss, Vanderbilt and other powerhouses in the
south.

Apparently, there were college scouts at the tournament
after all, because a couple of weeks after the tourney was over
I received a tremendously exciting phone call. The phone call
was from an assistant coach from the University of New
Orleans, also known as UNO. The coach told me how much
he loved to watch me play shortstop and how strong of a
player I was, the typical things a coach says to try to get you
to come to their school. He also said that besides seeing me
play in Jackson, another scout from UNO saw me at the East
Coast Pro and when all the staff got together for evaluations,
they all had me picked as their next shortstop. Wow!

He was telling me how great I would fit into the lineup
at UNO and how he was excited to pencil me in as the starting
shortstop for UNO. I was so excited to hear from a division I
school in the south, so part of my dream was coming true.
UNO played in a fairly strong conference called the Sunbelt
that has teams such as FIU, FAU, Middle Tennessee and
Western Kentucky. I honestly didn't care what conference
UNO was in because the coach wanted me so badly and I
wanted to play in the south.

I was a little scared, but I was excited about the possibility
of playing at UNO. As excited as we were, we also wanted to
keep our options open. The coach called from UNO on a
Friday night in August to say that on Saturday morning the
head coach would call me with my scholarship offer. The call
never came.

On Saturday, August 27th, 2005, Hurricane Katrina put
UNO underwater and destroyed most of New Orleans; this

was considered the worst and most tragic hurricane of the century. There were many casualties and broken lives and I could only imagine what happened to the coach and his team. My dreams and hopes of playing baseball at UNO were taken away. I had to put the University of New Orleans behind me and move on. Now I was getting more stressed and nervous because senior year was approaching and I still was not committed to a school.

My father came up with another approach to finding a college for me after he spoke to Neil Somers. He said that Florida had the best division 1 community college circuit and I had the ability to play there. I also knew of a pitcher that was on one of my showcase teams that went to Manatee Community College in Bradenton, FL (now called the State College of Florida). It was the best 'JUCO' (2 year baseball program) in the country. We looked into the school and found out it was 10 minutes from my mom's cousins, Gail and Ron Dickerson. Wow – wouldn't that be great to go to school in FL and have family there! We didn't know too much about the school or the coaches, but it didn't matter because we had to act fast before I had no college to attend. My dad called the coach at Manatee Community College and asked if he needed a shortstop next year, which he did, but he had to see me play. Perfect Game® we said! Let's find a Perfect Game tournament in FL for the fall. We called the LI Titans, another Long Island travel team that had a team going to the tournament, and Jim Clark, who was creating the roster for the Titans said he needed a shortstop – perfect fit. Coach Hill from Manatee drove 3 hours across the state of FL to see me play. On the last day of the showcase, he came up to me after the game and asked me questions about baseball and wanted to know how my grades were. I said all the right things. Later that week, the coach offered me a scholarship to play for him. It was such a load off my mind to know that I finally had a legitimate offer from a school in the south. It wasn't a division I four year school, but it was a well respected baseball school that wanted me and was located in a warm weather climate. By October of my senior year the search was over. My parents and I finally got into a successful baseball school in the south.

◆ CHAPTER FIVE ◆

The Cloudy First Year in the Sunshine State

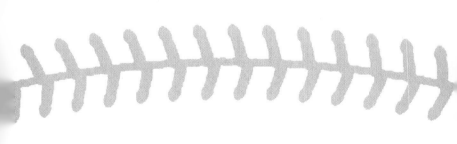

I didn't quite know what to expect coming out of high school and going into junior college. Manatee didn't have a real college atmosphere with football games and cheerleaders; it was a small 'juco' that had a fantastic baseball program. Since I was only 18 years old, I was young and naive when I arrived at Manatee. I was also a little cocky as well, since the Phillies wanted me out of high school. After I put in my time in junior college, I would be eligible to be drafted again. I knew I was good enough to play at Manatee and then move on to the minors.

I was wrong in so many ways. My competition at shortstop my first year was a player who I thought couldn't move left to right or field a ball as well as me. It didn't matter to our coach because the player was a hotshot transfer from the University of Louisville. I didn't think much of that shortstop's baseball ability. I thought that I could easily beat him out for the job. I was dead wrong, because at the end of the fall season, Coach Hill said that he earned his spot at shortstop and would be starting. I could not believe my ears when he said that. I thought I was so much better than him at all levels of the game, but I think I didn't start at shortstop because I was a freshman and wasn't ready to take on the challenges and responsibility that came with the position.

During practices throughout the fall, I played a little bit of every position since the other shortstop was going to be the starter. I played short, third base, leftfield and centerfield. Another reason why he started over me, in my opinion, was because Coach Hill liked the way he approached the baseball. He attacked the baseball and was aggressive, while I would usually sit back on the ball and wait for it. (*I remember that my travel ball coach, Don Whiston, used to try and get me to come in - but I was too stubborn to listen*). Coach Hill said that there are too many fast players at the junior college level and that I needed to 'come get the ball' more than I did. Coach Hill felt like I was not quite ready to play shortstop at the division 1 junior college level. He was right.

Coach Hill did eventually find a place for me to play— outfield. I could not believe that I was in the outfield. I've never played there in my life, but I knew that I could do it. I was considered a utility player for the fall season until I could earn a spot. At the beginning of the spring, I finally earned a position. The position was leftfield. Leftfield is the worst position to play on the field. You don't get many balls hit to you and you don't have to be talented at all to play there, but I had to shut my mouth and go with the flow.

Our first game of the season was an away game at Indian River Community College, and I was penciled in the starting lineup at leftfield. I was not happy about playing there, but I was thrilled to be in the opening day starting lineup. As we were getting loose and warming up for the game, one of the pitchers asked, "Hey, has anyone seen the Fungo bats?" (Fungo bats are practice bats for coaches) I didn't think anything of it because I don't care about Fungo bats and pitchers. A couple of minutes later, my buddy comes out to leftfield where I'm shagging balls and said, "Bobby, I think you were supposed to bring the bats." I told him, "No, I was put in charge of the towels for the trip." I was starting to get nervous because now we had no Fungo bats and Coach Hill had to borrow a bat from the other team, which was very embarrassing for him.

After we finished practicing, I was utterly exhausted and nervous at the same time. I walked down the dugout to the lineup card and the name HANEY had an enormous 'X' through it. I was scratched out from the opening day starting lineup for forgetting to bring the bats. I was about ready to cry in the dugout right then and there. I felt terrible during the national anthem and got ready to sit the bench.

Right before the game started, my Grandpa Bill and his wife Patti were in Florida and came by to see me play. My grandfather introduced himself and said to Coach Hill, "Hi, I'm Bobby Haney's Grandfather and I'm down here to watch him play." Coach Hill turned to my grandfather and said, "Sorry, Bobby has been scratched from the lineup for responsibility reasons." My grandpa is still mad at Coach Hill to this day for that incident. The whole situation was my fault.

I felt so embarrassed that whole day because I made my coaches look terrible, I made my team look pathetic, I made my grandpa look bad and worst of all, I made myself look like a complete idiot who couldn't bear any responsibility and remember to bring the Fungo bats. After the game was over I was dreading to talk to my grandpa because I knew he was upset that I didn't play. My grandpa loves to watch me play more than anyone else does. I told him the situation about forgetting the bats and how it was my responsibility. He understood everything, but he thought that my punishment was way too harsh. It was not a pleasant way to start the season and my college career. You are supposed to learn from your mistakes, and I learned from that one. From there on out, I made sure to triple check the list of things that I needed to bring on the road trips—no more being scratched from the lineup card.

As the season continued, I was stuck in leftfield and out of my element, which was the infield. The only time that I played shortstop or third base was when a player was suspended or didn't feel well. It was so difficult to stay focused during my first year of college because I came from a small town in New York where I was a superstar, and I was always considered one of the best players. Being drafted apparently didn't mean as much to my coach at junior college as it did me. I was a 'draft and follow' in high school, which meant that my scout was going to have another scout watch me throughout junior college. In the middle of the season, the Phillies scout came to me and told me that they couldn't redraft me since I wasn't playing at my primary position, shortstop. This made me even more upset because I felt as if my coach was going to destroy my career for good.

During the season when I got the chance to play, I took advantage of it. To make matters worse in my mind, the starting shortstop for us made more errors at short than I thought I would ever make, and had the same batting average as me. I felt his defense was just not as good as mine and I felt that some of his errors cost us games. I couldn't believe my eyes and still didn't understand why he was still playing shortstop. I was so frustrated inside because I knew that I should have been playing short.

When my parents came down to visit me during the season, I told my father that I wanted to quit playing baseball. I told him, "Look, if I can't even start over the shortstop here, then how am I ever going to play at the next level?" I will never forget what my dad told me after that. He said, "Look, Bobby, you're still young. You are only 18 and have so many more years of baseball left. Just keep your head up and stay positive." I tried to apply what he said to my baseball career, and it helped a lot. Even though I sat the bench and played outfield most of my freshman year, it was still a good experience. In the long run, you just have to win ball games and stop complaining about where you are playing or how much playing time you're getting. I had to stay focused and look toward my long-term goals, rather than dwell on the short term.

Once again, my father had given me excellent advice and he was right. I had to focus and stay positive because I was still young and I had so many more games and 'at bats' left in my career. Looking back today, I think I was crazy for telling my father that I wanted to quit. It goes back to the saying, "When life gives you lemons, you should go ahead and make some lemonade." I was playing outfield and I had to make the best of it. I had to be thankful that I was getting 'at bats' and playing most of the time. I am one of those people who thinks that not only does everything happen for a reason, it happens for a positive reason. When something happens to you, look at the positive side of it and not the negative.

Whether I played outfield, infield or sat the bench, I made sure I was not wasting my time. My father always told me to absorb all you can from the coaches when I was sitting on the bench. During practice, he said to pick their brains and ask them questions. My dad always told me to learn something new and get better at the game I love. When I would sit the bench, I would talk to people and ask some of the assistant coaches questions about the game. I absorbed all of the advice and pointers I could and became a better player for it.

Sometimes I would only get an at bat when the game was on the line in the seventh inning, so I always made sure to stay loose and hit in the practice cage during the game. Some of us would play this game in the batting cage where we would hit off the tee and hit a spot on the net for a certain amount of points. This game helped us to not only stay relaxed, but also helped us to hit line drives and maintain a proper swing and approach to the baseball. If I couldn't get better on the field, then I was going to do it on the bench or in the cage. I was just not going to sit on the bench and have a negative attitude and learn nothing. When the shortstop made an error or hit a home run, I would pat him on the butt and tell him to shake it off or congratulate him, whatever the situation demanded. I had to become a valued team leader and a positive guy when sitting the bench.

I took the first year at Manatee as a learning experience and knew that I had to become stronger physically and mentally. I needed to have much more confidence in myself and have more responsibility. I knew that I had to be more aggressive when fielding the baseball. I had to attack it rather than sit back on it. I knew I had to go back home and work on some things I had learned throughout the year.

When I went back to New York, I played the summer with the Long Island Titans. We played strong competition and traveled to East Cobb, GA, for one of our tournaments. It was an enjoyable time playing with those guys, and we were a hard team to beat. During that summer season, I was getting looks from Penn State, even though I still had a scholarship with Manatee Community College. The Long Island Titans team that I was on wondered why I didn't start at shortstop at Manatee and thought that the school was not the right fit for me. Everyone thought that I should go ahead and sign with Penn State and not return to Manatee. My travel coach wanted me to go to Penn State because he knew that they were building a new facility and Manatee was just a junior college.

My father went to Penn State, so I thought he was going to be thrilled that I got an offer. It turned out he didn't care because he wanted what was best for me, and that was to play in the warm climate in Florida. My dad was right again. One of the Penn State coaches called me up and told me that they were building a new stadium and that they would give me a pretty decent scholarship. I knew that if I signed with Penn State, there would be no more baseball in Florida and no more beautiful beaches. I knew if I signed with Penn State that Coach Hill would be extremely unhappy. I just had to remain patient and stay focused. I knew that Manatee was going to be the right way to go and that my second year was going to be much different.

After we lost our first game in the College World Series to OU, we had to stay alive. So the next game we took our anger out on ASU with our bats.

Photo by Juan Blas/TheBigSpur.com

That's me in fifth grade with my best friend Vincent Liang. We loved the game and dominated in our age group.

Photo by Jeff Haney

When I was little, my eyes lit up when someone threw me a baseball or even said the word baseball. It was like asking a dog if they wanted to go for a walk.

Photo by Jeff Haney

I even try to make sure I look like Jeter when I fly through the air on a double play.

Photo by Juan Blas/TheBigSpur.com

Photo by Alana Buckley

We never go anywhere
without each other.
Here are my friends and
I tailgating at a Yankee
game. A classic day well
spent in the Bronx.

I may have struggled in the
batters box in college, but
in high school, I crushed
everything.

Photo by Richard Valeo, Huntington, NY

Our Clemson rival games were so intense that they shot out smoke from both dugouts to introduce the players.

Photo by Juan Blas/TheBigSpur.com

Sometimes it was so hot during the State Tournament in Junior College, we played games in our practice shirts.

Photo by Andy Gregory

One of my favorite pictures of 'my boys' and I. Nick, Myself, Rob Ted, from left to right.

Photo by Lauren Romano.

I'm proud of my high school plaque, which sits next to the plaques of other baseball standouts such as Coach Duke Durland, John Dekams, and Houston Astro Craig Biggio, who played at Kings Park in the 1980's.

BOBBY HANEY
BASEBALL
· ALL STATE 2005, 2006
· LEAGUE MVP 2005, 2006
· GOLD GLOVE 2005, 2006
CAREER LEADER
AB - 288   H - 121   R - 100   2B - 24
HR - 11   RBI - 81   AVE. - .420
TOTAL BASES - 192

I tried to model myself after Derek Jeter in anyway I could. Especially the way I stood in the infield before I played a game.

In high school I could hit as good a any other shortstop. But it was m defense that separated me from the res

Photo by Mary Ellen Gambardella

Photo by Bill Han

My Grandma JoAnn and Grandpa Bob have always supported me and flew out to see me in the World Series in Omaha.

Photo by Brandon Haney

My Florida family, Gail & Ron, from Bradenton, always took time to watch me play.

Photos by Jeff Haney

Minutes after we won the championship I was presented with this gold watch and then I walked over to the stands and gave it to my Dad. We were both emotionally drained.

My Grandpa Haney and his wife Patti. Grandpa would attend more high school baseball games than anyone I ever met. Grandpa loves the game and was always so proud to see me play, especially at the final game in Omaha.

Shown here at the Univ. of Georgia are my Grandma Haney, (who was always on
top of me for my grades), and Uncle Rick and Aunt Debbie (Haneys from Georgia)
who have been great supporters of my college and pro career. My Cousins
Jonathan, Caela & Rebecca (GA) & Mike Kahn (from Maryland) made the trip also!

Top and
upper right
photos by
Jeff Haney

My beautiful girlfriend Danielle and her family always supported me throughout my baseball career
as well. Shown with Danielle are her Dad Dennis, Mom Kelly and younger brother Denny.

Photo by Ragosta Fam.

There is no family in the world as close as we are. They are my best support group and have made a difference throughout my career. Left to right: Top Row: Dad, Brother Brandon, Grandpa Bob far right. Middle Row: Josh, Uncle Rob, Sammi, Brother Brian, Grandma JoAnn and me. Bottom Row: Aunt Mary Ellen, Justin, Mom, Aunt Ann Marie, Christopher and Uncle Kevin. Bottom Photo: My Family.

Photo by Bill Haney

Photo by Brandon Haney

One of my favorite pictures. My teammates help me hoist the National Championship Trophy after the final win in Rosenblatt history.

Believe me - it's a dream come true to see your name and photo up in lights at Rosenblatt. Nothing else compares.

Photo by Gaines DuVall Sports Portraits

Photo by Juan Blas/TheBigSpur.com

I finally felt like a pro with my firs ever professional baseball card wit the San Francisco Giant

Photo by Juan Blas/TheBigSpur.com

Every young baseball player's dream is to dog pile
after the final game of the College World Series
in Rosenblatt Stadium.™

Photo by Danielle Ragosta.

My Mom, MaryAnne and
Dad, Jeff, shown with my
Gold Glove award after the
first ever SC ring ceremony,
Fall of 2010, in South Carolina.

My very supportive and loving
girlfriend (Pookie) and I spending a
night in the Hampton's.

Photo by Mary Ellen Gambardella

◆ CHAPTER SIX ◆

You Never Know Who's Watching

It would have been a bad decision to transfer to another school and a difficult thing to do as far as my degree program went, because there are always problems with credits transferring over from different schools. It would have looked terrible on my part if I left Manatee without giving the school another chance. My second year at Manatee was a complete change from my first year. I felt more mature because I knew how the baseball program was conducted, and I was now a sophomore. The shortstop from the previous season graduated from Manatee and proceeded on to the University of Tampa. I was now the starting shortstop, and it was my spot to lose. I was extremely excited because I was finally back in my position where I thought I belonged. We had a highly promising team, and we were going to compete for a shot at the Junior College World Series in Grand Junction, Colorado.

When you're in junior college, you play games in the fall season against other teams in your conference. If you go to a division I school, you can only play games against your own teammates. Playing in the fall in juco helps your chances of being recruited by a DI school. During fall baseball at Manatee, I was hoping to get recruited by a division I school in Florida. I always wanted to play for Florida, and it was a part of my dream to be a Gator. During the fall season at Manatee, I played hard and tried to get picked up by a college or possibly get drafted again. I received a couple of calls from schools such as Barry University, Tampa University and Elon University. Elon heavily recruited me and wanted me to come in and play shortstop. Barry was interested, but I only spoke to the coach one time. Tampa University was a highly successful division II school that I was excited about, but I really didn't want to go to a division II school. Even though Tampa won the NCAA Division II National Championship a couple of years in a row, there was still nothing like a division

I school. There is no competition between the two divisions as far as talent goes, so I knew I had to make it to a division I college no matter what.

The assistant coach at Manatee, Al Corbeil, was a legend at Manatee and at Florida International University. He was our hitting coach and bench coach. He also set just about every record in the offensive category as a player and was a catcher. He played a few years in pro ball and had injuries here and there. Coach Corbeil was also close friends with the pitching coach at the University of South Carolina, Mark Calvi. Mark Calvi was a coach at FIU when Corbeil played there. Coach Ray Tanner and South Carolina have been recruiting players from junior colleges for many years. Junior college players who transfer to USC usually turn out to be prominent players and go on to play professional baseball. The shortstop at South Carolina, Reese Havens, was a junior when I was at Manatee, and Reese was predicted to be a first round draft pick and leave after his junior year. Coach Corbeil told Coach Calvi from USC that he had a pretty decent shortstop looking to sign with a division I school.

When Coach Calvi came down to Florida, he was in need of a couple of pitchers and a shortstop. I had no clue that Coach Calvi was scouting me to come play at USC. I saw a scout standing around the field during a couple of games that I played in. During one game at Pasco Hernando Community College, he was standing right behind the backstop. Going up to the plate, I felt that the scout was watching my every move and knew this was my chance to shine. I had runners in scoring position, but I struck out to end the inning. I was utterly embarrassed, but it was still early in the game. The next at bat, the scout was still looking on, and I crushed a run double into the left center field gap. I was feeling a lot better about myself after that at bat. I continued to play stellar defense throughout the game and finished up 2 for 5, with a couple of runs batted in.

After the game was over, the scout was waiting for me outside the fence as we were about to head to the bus. He approached me and said, "Hi, I'm Mark Calvi with the University of South Carolina." When I heard that and saw his hat had the Gamecocks logo printed on it, I thought, "Wow, is this actually happening right now?" I was thrilled, but acted like I had been in the situation a million times. Coach Calvi said something that I will never forget. With a big smile he asked, "How would you like to play for the Gamecocks?" At first, I didn't know what to say, but I was thrilled and told him yes.

I was barely getting recruited to play at any of the top schools in the country, and now South Carolina came into the picture. Coach Calvi told me about the shortstop situation and about Reese Havens becoming a first rounder. The Cocks needed me, and I needed them as well. I didn't even know what conference South Carolina played in; I was from New York and didn't know anything about big universities in the south. I asked Coach Calvi what conference USC was in and he told me that South Carolina played in the SEC. I thought he said the SCC, so obviously I didn't know much about college sports. I was excited about the opportunity and couldn't wait to tell my parents on the bus ride back to Manatee that evening.

After Coach Calvi and I met that evening at Pasco Hernando, he wanted to meet with me again at our home field in Bradenton. He was there to watch me practice and to watch a couple of our pitchers throw bullpens. When he talked to me before practice, he told me to have fun and hit some balls over the fence during batting practice. Sure enough, that practice was my best one of the year. I was fielding every ground ball and making highlight reel plays at short, while having the best batting practice of my life. I was hitting balls off the light poles and over the scoreboard. It was as if God was swinging the bat for me at the time.

After the practice was over, Coach Calvi was waiting for me again to go over a couple of things. We discussed scholarship offers and talked about me taking an official visit up to USC. The scholarship offer was only around 35 percent because I was a middle infielder and they needed me to sign early. I asked Coach Calvi how early I would have to make my decision and he said in the next couple of nights. I was surprised at how quickly I would have to make the decision, but knew that I would be going to South Carolina.

Over the next couple of days, we were playing Lake City Community College and before the game, I told my Dad that I wanted to commit to USC and I did! Coach Calvi was there once again, and when I got off the bus in Lake City before the game, he said, "I heard the good news, congratulations!" I said, "Yup, thanks a lot, Coach." Coach Calvi told me he hoped I had a good game and wished me luck. In that game at Lake City with Coach Calvi watching, I went 5 for 5 at the plate and made every play in the field. I guess you can say it was meant to be. I was destined to be a Gamecock. I couldn't wait to go on my official USC visit and see the campus.

I thought I was a hotshot at Manatee because I was the first one to commit to a massive powerhouse division I baseball school. I could now sit back and relax because I didn't have to worry about where I was going to school for the next couple of months.

A few weeks later, I had my official visit and flew into Columbia, South Carolina. Another junior college player named Justin Dalles also came on the visit with me. He was a catcher from St. Petersburg Community College. On the visit, we got a tour of the entire campus, including the 'Strom' where all the college students go to work out, and we drove by the site where the new Carolina baseball stadium was going to be built. We were treated very well and I loved every minute of it. I went to my first college football game and watched the Gamecocks play Tim Tebow and the Florida Gators. The atmosphere was awesome, but the game was a blowout. The Gamecocks got killed and Tebow scored five touchdowns by himself. It was a thrilling experience and a substantial change from the small community college I attended. I couldn't wait to go to USC and play baseball against the top schools in the country.

During the spring of my sophomore year at Manatee, I was off to a slow start, just like all my seasons, but then I started to heat up. I was hitting above .400 at the time and was tied with the school's all time hitting streak. I was going at least 2 for 5 every game it seemed and I was hoping to get drafted. I thought I would easily get drafted high because I was committed to USC and was playing exceptionally well. After we lost to Chipola Community College in the state tournament, our season was over. We were devastated, but I knew I had my whole career ahead of me.

A month after the state tournament, I received phone calls from several different scouts right before the draft. I got calls from the Cardinals, the Mets, the Blue Jays and a few other teams. The scouts that were in the stands during my sophomore year were there just to see me and nobody else. There was one incident that happened during a game we played in Tampa, when a Mets scout was there, and I deeply regretted it. I hit a ground ball to second and ran a 5.6 down to first base – very slow and lazy. After that, the Mets scout told Coach Tim Hill that I was off his list for now because I hadn't run hard enough. When my coach told me that, I was upset. I knew I made a mistake and took the game for granted.

I knew that moving forward I had to play hard all the time and never relax while playing. It was my wake-up call.

Right before the draft in June, the Mets called me again and invited me to a pre-draft workout across the state in Port St. Lucie. The scouts were very courteous to my father previously on the phone and at the workout they seemed particularly interested in me. When I arrived, I felt old, as almost every kid there was in high school or was a freshman in junior college. I had a decent workout that day and after the workout, one of the scouts asked me how much it would take for me to sign with them. I said I would probably sign for about $100,000, but no less because I was committed to one of the best schools in the country for baseball. The scout said, "I don't know about that amount, but I could see you going in the 25th round." After hearing that from the scout, I was not too happy. When the workout was over, the scouts told us that we would get a call before the draft and would be in touch. The day before the draft, we didn't receive a single phone call and my family and I were wondering what was going on. The first day of the draft came and went and nothing happened—I wasn't drafted and didn't receive a single phone call. The second day went by and we heard nothing again. I never got a call from the Mets, not one phone call saying anything about my status either way. My father was very mad because the scouts acted like they loved me and said that they were going to call us. We did learn that the Mets drafted the South Carolina Shortstop, Reese Havens. Everyone also knew that I was going to SC to replace him. My dad figured that something was 'up' and we were not getting drafted. We had to get over that and just put it behind us. It was time to start focusing on playing baseball in the SEC and stepping up my game to the next level.

Toward the end of my junior college playing career, my

buddy on the team, Taylor Hashman, was dating a girl from Florida named Lauren and she had a cousin that was just coming out of a relationship. Danielle and I started to date at Manatee and we are still together to this day. It's not easy to juggle baseball, school and a girlfriend – but Danielle helps me get through the daily stresses of the game and I'm glad I have her. She is the love of my life and another great thing about playing ball in the south!

◆ CHAPTER SEVEN ◆

First Year as a Gamecock

I didn't know what to expect during my first year in Columbia, South Carolina. Everything was a complete change from junior college. The people, the coaches, the girls and the professors all seemed very different from Manatee Community. The baseball program and the new Carolina Stadium were also very different, but in a good way. When I arrived in late August for the start of my junior year, the stadium was under construction and it was one of the main reasons that I signed with USC. Even though it would not be completed until December, we were allowed to practice on it starting in September.

It took a little time to adapt to USC because there were more rules and restrictions. There were more students and fans to deal with, which was a little overwhelming at first. We had no press to worry about in Manatee, but we had to give interviews at USC and had to be careful about what we said. The fan base at USC was so large, and you had people following your status on Facebook, so it was important to be careful about what you said as I was now a role model for so many. Even though it took a little time to get adjusted, it felt comforting knowing that I had the support of one of the best college fan bases in the country.

I was so nervous on the first day of fall practice. I was trying to replace a first round shortstop, Reese Havens. I knew I couldn't look at it that way, and that I just had to stay focused and play my game, but it was difficult knowing I had some big shoes to fill. The first day was scary because I didn't know where to go when I got to the field, and everyone was already hitting and fielding. I heard Coach Tanner say, "Haney, let's go, hurry up," which did nothing to ease my nerves. I couldn't just take my time and relax because I didn't know how the program was run yet. I had to listen to Coach Tanner and do everything that he wanted in order for me to learn the ropes at Carolina.

The first day of practice was so hot. I spent all summer in New York, and now I was in "The armpit of the south." The humidity level in South Carolina is always high, especially at the end of the summer, and it can be almost unbearable at times. After a round of infield, I was out of breath and Coach Tanner was making fun of me, saying I was out of shape and not ready. I was laughing, but I was also nervous because I was exhausted and it was embarrassing that the head coach saw me like this. As we practiced more and more, I got used to the heat and humidity.

When we moved to the new baseball field for practice, I felt like I was playing in Yankee Stadium. The field at Carolina Stadium was perfect in every way that you could imagine. The grass was cut perfectly. There were no lips on the infield and the sun was never in your line of vision. Everything was done perfectly, from the scoreboard to the stands. When I took my first ground ball on the new field, it was like playing on carpet. It seemed almost impossible to make a fielding error.

Some other great features of the stadium included a brand new weight room, a mini kitchen to eat in, a new training room with a lot more training tables and a giant indoor batting facility. The best thing the baseball stadium had to offer to us players was the locker room. The locker room was enormous with an incredible sound system that shook the building on game day. We had three flat screen TVs surrounding us and a brand new bathroom with showers connected to it. I didn't feel like we deserved this because it was almost over the top. We felt so spoiled with the new stadium, but that was just the beginning. Coming from a junior college into this I thought I was dreaming. Our locker room at junior college was the size of our bathroom at USC. We were provided with plenty of baseball clothes, cleats, batting gloves, sweat-suits and much more. We had a bat for batting practice and another bat for the game. I felt like I was in the big leagues! We got to order our own infielders gloves customized in whatever color we wanted. There were certainly not going to be any equipment excuses for poor play. We had everything you could want to play the game and play it right!

As the semester carried on, I was introduced to all the school activities that students went to, such as the football games, bars and Five Points. As a baseball player, you are the big man on campus since you play at a major university with one of the best baseball programs in the country. It was very different from the atmosphere at a junior college. Everyone wanted to know me, hang out with me and be a part of Carolina baseball. It would have been a lot of fun to go to South Carolina as a regular student, but it was even better for me to go as a baseball player. The teachers knew who you were in the classroom and the other students always asked if you played baseball or not. I loved getting attention and I loved it at USC.

Football games are the best part of the fall. People from Columbia and from all over South Carolina, plus fans of other schools pile in on Saturdays to watch the game. Tailgating at a college football game is the best because you just sit and relax with a cold beverage in your hand while the warm autumn sun shines on your face. I never usually went into the stadium to see the game. I enjoyed the tailgate atmosphere and watched the game on a Flatscreen. Sitting with 80,000 screaming fans is not my thing. The football games are always well attended. On game days – the girls wear these beautiful black dresses and look fantastic! I had heard about how nice the girls look at other SEC schools, but in my opinion the best looking girls go to SC!

The University of South Carolina offers great academics, sports, and of course social life. There are many good restaurants and bars at Five Points – where many students hang out. If you are under the drinking age, you hang at a house party. The best party of the year is the Halloween party that the baseball team has with plenty of refreshments and dancing. Everyone has a good time. As a student athlete, we are always watching what we do and say and we try very hard to stay out of trouble. Just like at any other college – kids can get out of control sometimes. It's important to always do the right thing, look after your friends, and respect the program and the coaches that you represent.

South Carolina does not have any professional teams, so playing baseball for USC is like playing in the pros. I thought it was so cool when we had to sign autographs for the fans right before the football game during the fall. The fans treated us so great and were happy to be a part of everything we did. The big difference between playing at a small junior college and playing at a major division I school are the distractions. People are always trying to get you to do stuff, like sign an autograph, take a picture or buy you food. You have to be careful not to break any NCAA rules or you could find yourself suspended for a certain amount of games. You are under a microscope when you play at a significant DI school and are considered to be a mini-celebrity, so you have to watch out for people who could get you into trouble, whether it is intentional or not. Some people might act as if they are your best friend, but sometimes those same people might love to see you lose your scholarship as well.

Most people have no idea what it's like to be a student athlete at a division 1 school. Some people might think it's easy – classes, sports, what could be hard? Let me tell you that balancing your academics with a sport is much harder to do than you might think. When you play baseball for example at a top university it sometimes seems harder than a full-time job!

You are always busy no matter what, and at the same time, you are not even being paid to do any of it. You may get a partial college scholarship, but that isn't much money in the grand scheme of things. People don't seem to realize that when you are a student athlete, you have to work extra hard on your schoolwork. You have to balance both school and baseball at the same time. If you don't maintain a certain GPA throughout school, then you are not allowed to play sports and you could lose your scholarship.

Playing baseball and keeping up my grades was not an easy thing for me. Our regular schedule is to wake up in the morning at about 8:00, eat a nourishing meal and go to class until about noon. After classes, you eat a decent lunch, then practice at 2:00, lift weights at 5:00 and go to study hall from 7:00 to 9:00. After all that is done, you have to find a way to cook yourself a good dinner because athletes have to eat healthy meals. Then the next day, we have to start all over again, just like a normal workday from 9:00 to 5:00, except we have to put in more hours. Keeping up with everything can be difficult, especially if you are trying to be a decent student and a good athlete at the same time.

Sometimes my teammates and I would get frustrated because of our difficult schedule, but then we would stop and realize that we are doing it all because we love to play the game of baseball. We all have a passion for the game. During the fall semester, the only thing I had to do was play decent in the intersqaud games and get decent grades in order to play in the springtime. If you can't pass your classes with decent grades, then there is no springtime baseball for you. No athlete enjoys going to class every day, and that is why we always look forward to 2:00, when baseball practice starts. Almost every day I would show up to practice and Coach Tanner would always ask me how my grades were. He would say, "Haney,

how ya grades?" No matt
were fine. Then he woul
aren't, then it's back witl
Tanner always made su
strong in the fall in orde
us had it easier than othe
For example, some majo
others pursued sociolog
GPA at the end of the fa
the spring.

please everyone becau
in the classroom an
not producing o
on you big ti
producing
your te
is ab

The great thing about being a student athlete is that you can get help whenever you need it with any subject. Tutors were always there for us when we need them. As student athletes, we try to take advantage of that privilege as much as we can because we spend so much time on the baseball field. Sometimes it is just so hard to focus in school when all you keep thinking about is Carolina baseball. There was not a day that went by when I would be sitting in class thinking about going to Omaha, Nebraska. I would be in class writing notes and doodling on my paper the words "OMAHA." That's all I could ever think about when I was in school and that was the only thing that mattered to me at the time. Even though Omaha was the ultimate goal that my teammates and I had, I had to try to keep that in the back of my mind and focus on schoolwork, but that was easier said than done sometimes. When I look back at college and high school, I don't think that I put enough effort into my studies. My parents always said that I was a '90' student doing '80' work. Being a 'C' student did not help me or my coaches. The last thing that a coach wants is a good ballplayer with bad grades. It's not good for anybody. I should have worked harder. I could have been a better student.

As a college baseball player, it is exceedingly difficult to

se you are trying to get decent grades
d produce on the field as well. If you are
n the field, then the fans and the coaches are
ne, which is expected, of course. If you are not
in the classroom, then your coaches, your parents,
chers and your academic advisor are on your case. It
most impossible to fail a class at Carolina because there
e so many people that stay on top of you and try to help you
out. It is an extremely long baseball season come springtime,
with up to 70 games if you make it to Omaha. You have to
juggle your tests on Fridays when we leave for road trips on
Thursdays, and you have to stay on top of your homework. It
seemed like we rarely got any time for ourselves.

It was more important for me to get an 'A' on a test than
it was to get three hits in a game because grades are just that
important. If you go 4 for 4 in a game and then get a 70 on a
test the next day, you're going to study your tail off for the next
test. My ultimate motivation as a student was knowing that if
I didn't do well in my classes, then I would not be able to play
in the spring. I would be letting down my team, my family
and myself. During my first fall semester, I was just getting
by with making mostly C's and a couple D's, which was not
acceptable. I was on the verge of not being able to play in
the spring. I had to have a GPA of a 1.9 and I barely had that
because my grades at the end of the semester were pathetic.
My grades averaged out to be a 1.8, and I knew that I was
going to be in serious trouble with my parents and with Coach
Tanner. In one of the classes that I received a C in, I thought
that I should have had a B in that class. The professor said he
gave me a C because I exceeded the maximum number of
absences allowed, which dropped my grade. I went to the class
all the time, so I knew that I didn't have too many absences.
If you're an athlete, there are people in the class that check to

see if the athletes go to class. My academic advisor and I contacted the head guy who appoints the class checkers, and we looked back at his records. I told my academic advisor that I didn't miss that number of classes. He believed me and sure enough, the guy in charge of class checking said I was right. I never had as many absences as were on record. My grade was then changed from a C to a B and that raised my GPA to a 2.0. I put my family and my coach through a bumpy and stressful ride, but at least I was eligible to play in the spring. My father always said that I did not 'play the game' in the classroom. He said that I needed to figure out how to succeed in class and do things to raise my grade. He was right. I could have participated more and had a better relationship with my professors. You have to realize that you might never take this class again – so get the most out of it. And – don't forget that these classes cost money – most likely my parents money.

The reason Coach Tanner was so scared that I was not going to be eligible during the spring was because I was pretty much the only guy who could play shortstop. At the beginning of all the fall practices, each player had to meet on the field at certain times, and I had to go in the later part of the day. When I took my position on the field for practice, I quickly noticed something. I noticed that there were not any cleat marks or imprints of shoes anywhere by the shortstop position. No one was practicing or playing shortstop except for me. I was the only guy at the shortstop position at the time. There were other guys on the team who could probably play the position, but Coach Tanner didn't think so, which is why he had no one else practicing at the spot. When they tell you before you commit to a college that you're going to play a certain position, something might change like in junior college when I played leftfield. Coach Mark Calvi and Coach Ray Tanner stuck to their idea of me at the shortstop position.

I was so excited and truly honored that I was going to be the shortstop on opening day in the new Carolina Stadium.

After the fall was over and done with, I was excited and felt like a massive weight was lifted off my back. I was eligible to play, and opening day for Carolina Stadium was finally here. Darius Rucker from Hootie and the Blowfish sang the national anthem to start off the 2009 baseball season. When the first pitch was thrown on my debut at South Carolina, a strike was called by the umpire. I couldn't believe how loud that crowd was on the first pitch of the game. I come from a small town in New York where we are lucky if 50 fans make it to the game. This place was roaring with more than 9,000 fans in attendance. I was nervous and excited at the same time. I was ready for a ball to be hit to me, and I wanted to get the first one out of the way quick. There were two outs in the first, and sure enough, there was a ground ball hit right at me. I fielded it cleanly and threw the guy out at first for the final out of the inning. The butterflies were gone and the season had begun. At the plate, I could not work things out on the first game. I went 0 for 4 on opening day with an RBI. The next day I went 3 for 4 and was finally on the board.

We had a better season than many people thought we would have. A lot of the coaches and the sports analysts didn't think we were going to have a good season because the stud players from the 2008 season were drafted. Justin Smoak was gone, Reese Havens was gone, James Darnell was gone and the clutch hitting Phil Disher was gone. Honestly, the team and I were sick of hearing about those guys and people wondering how we were going to manage to play without them. There was always a question in an interview when a reporter asked about one of the four studs who graduated. We had to play our game and win baseball games.

We ended up having a good season in 2009 and

made it to regionals, just like last year's team. Unfortunately, we had a tragic ending to our season when we traveled to East Carolina to face the Pirates. There were four teams in our regional: USC, ECU, Binghamton and George Mason. We flew by George Mason, beating them with no problem, and then we beat the host of the tournament, ECU, by a score of 12 to 2 in the next game. We were going strong, and all we needed to do was beat ECU one more time to advance to the Super Regionals. In the second game on Sunday night, ECU was destroying us 8 to 0. We came back scoring six epic runs with the tying run at second base, but failed to tie it up and lost.

The winner of the next game would advance to the Super Regionals—go big or go home! I had a couple of early hits, and we took an early 3-0 lead. We knocked out ECU's starting pitcher in the third inning after he gave up five runs. We were cruising, but knew that it wasn't over until it was over. ECU hit a two-run jack in the bottom of the fifth, which made the score 6-2. Later in the game, we scored and ECU scored twice, making the score 7-4. In the bottom of the seventh, ECU was hitting lasers and scored two runs, pulling them within one. In the eighth, we needed some insurance for sure, and Jackie Bradley Jr., also known as JBJ, provided it. Jackie hit a 2-run blast down the line in right to put us up 9 to 6. We were going nuts in the dugout and figured that the game was over.

Going into the bottom of the ninth inning we were still up by three. We were three outs away from clinching our spot in the Supers. The closer Farotto walked the first batter. Curtis Johnson, also known as Cujo, came in to shut the door. Cujo walked another guy, and then ECU's savior Devin Harris came to the plate. Cujo hung a pitch to Harris and Harris hit a long line drive shot over the stands in left center. The ball game was tied! After we got out of the heart-breaking inning, we

went to extras. The momentum was clearly in ECU's fav
but we had to fight back and score a run. We ended up
scoring in the tenth inning and had to hold ECU in the b
tom half. Once again, we gave up a couple of hits and walk
a couple. ECU had the winning run on 2nd base and De
Harris came up to the plate again. Harris drilled a seed ri
past me up the middle to score the walk off winning run
the stadium went nuts. We blew it and ECU was going
Supers. We never like to talk about how that season end
because we knew that we had so many chances, and we j
could not get it done. We played great in that regional, but
did ECU. It was just a shame that we were not the ones
come out on top. Someone has to win and someone has
lose, and unfortunately, it was us in 2009. That was a hea
breaker and something that we will never forget. We kn
that the 2009 season was finally behind us, and we had
forget about it. We had to hope that the 2010 season was go
to be different and that we would win it all.

Following the letdown of our regional, I found out t
I had to have surgery on my throwing shoulder. I star
having problems with my shoulder right after high school
always felt my bicep tighten up and it would feel hard as a ro
after I threw the ball. The reason why my bicep was so ti
was because my shoulder was weak, which caused me to u
my bicep more than I should have. My trainer said tha
had a small case of bicep tendonitis. The tendon that r
from my bicep to my shoulder was weak and it needed
be strengthened. I had to get my shoulder stronger, s
wouldn't have to feel pain or tightness in my bicep or shoul
anymore. I did all kinds of exercises in order to help ma
my arm stronger.

When I arrived at South Carolina, my throwing a
continued to hurt, and it was still from the bicep tendoni

After the season was over, my trainer insisted that I have shoulder surgery. I did not want to have the surgery, but this time it wasn't because I was scared of the pain; I was worried that the surgery would keep me from getting drafted. I had a long talk with my father and then talked it over with Coach Tanner, and they both agreed that I should go ahead with the surgery. I didn't think that it was smart to have surgery on my throwing shoulder going into my last year of college, but Coach Tanner convinced me to go ahead with it. He said if I got drafted and then had surgery in pro ball that I might end up getting released. Organizations don't like to have senior draftees get injured, so instead of paying for the surgery, they just release them. I didn't want that to happen to me, so I went along with Coach Tanner and my parents and agreed to the surgery, even if it did mean that I wouldn't get drafted that summer.

My mother and father wanted me to have the surgery where I lived in New York, but they wanted me to rehab back at SC and also enroll to take a summer class. With the advice of my dad's baseball advisor, Neil Somers, we had the surgery done by the best - Doctor David Dines, head doctor for the United States Tennis Association and former doc with the Mets. The doc said that my shoulder was not torn, but was about to tear, and that's why surgery was needed.

After I came out of surgery, I was in pain because I was not in a cast like my last surgery; my arm was only wrapped up and put in a sling. I took it slow because it was the summer time and the surgery was not a serious one. I had plenty of time to get back to where I needed to be, which was 100 percent by the end of the fall. In August before school started, I rehabbed my shoulder every single day at the Carolina football stadium, so the trainers there could keep an eye on me. When the fall came around, I still was not allowed to throw at all, so I just hit and fielded ground balls. My arm was getting there slowly but surely. At the end of the fall, I was on a throwing program and on my way to being 100 percent. Over the winter break, I worked to get my arm strong and back to the way it was before. After a lot of work, and dedication by USC staff, I was finally ready for my last year of college baseball and the 2010 season to get underway.

◆ CHAPTER EIGHT ◆

The National Championship

My experiences from my young days in the travel league to my two seasons at Manatee and two years at USC all led to a chance to be part of claiming a national title. After we finished off Clemson in classy fashion, with two straight wins to knock them out of playing for the championship, we were headed to the National Championship Series against UCLA. Some teams might have felt nervous, but we felt like our hard work was officially over. We paid our dues and were on cruise control from here on out, loose and relaxed. The way we felt going into the National Championship Series was whatever happened was just gravy, or icing on the cake.

No one ever really talked about this, but the night before game 1 of the championship series, our fire alarm went off in our hotel room at about 2:30 in the morning. I was so annoyed, but was also laughing at the time because I figured a UCLA fan pulled the alarm. We stood outside until 3:00 in the morning and then finally went back to bed. We had no problem getting up in a couple of hours for breakfast and pretended like nothing ever happen.

When we headed out of our hotel room that night, we were ready to play in the biggest game of our lives. We were so loose in the dugout before the game and messed around like usual. We had our work cut out for us as UCLA's stud pitcher Garret Cole was raring to go. We started out early in the game being aggressive and getting a little lucky.

In the first inning, with the spirit stick in the hands of one of our players, we scored two quick runs off Cole. We had some timely hits and also some lucky breaks. We scored on an error, and then we scored a run on a check swing single by Brady Thomas. We were finding ways to get it done early, and the rest was history because of one man on the mound. Blake Cooper didn't let his guard down all game and shut down the UCLA offense. I had a solid game with my share of hits and drove in three runs that night. I loved it afterwards, because I felt more relaxed and I was getting interviewed. I felt like a movie star that night on the big stage in Omaha, Nebraska. It all came down to this – we were one win away from winning the College World Series and only had 27 outs to go. We technically had two games to win the title, but wanted to get it done in one.

The next morning, we woke up knowing that we were one win away from winning it all. People ask me what was going through my head at the time, and I tell them just what I told the reporter after game 1. I said, "You just gotta play nice and loose and play the game of baseball like you are 12 years old again." Mickey Mantle always expressed that if you can't have fun playing this game, then something is wrong with you. I know it's easy for Mickey Mantle to say that, but he was right.

I will never forget what happened to me before we left the hotel to get on the bus. As I was leaving the lobby, I saw a woman and man standing at the doorway and the woman had a camera in her hand. She asked, "Can you take your glasses off your hat please?" I was wondering why she wanted me to take my glasses off, and then I realized that I had the initials B.T. written above the brim of my hat. The initials stood for Bayler Teal, who was a seven-and-a-half year old boy who passed from his battle with cancer on June 24, 2010, just five days earlier. I asked the woman, "Are you Bayler's mother?" She shook her head yes as her eyes started to turn into glass. I hugged her and said, "I'm so sorry. We are going to win it for him." Mrs. Teal wanted a picture of my hat and his initials. Bayler, who threw out the first pitch at one of our games back in the middle of the 2010 season, was a true Gamecock fan. After that moment, I played with a heavy heart and so did my teammates.

That night the entire country knew what position we were in and how fortunate we were. Before the game, we were looser than ever because all the pressure was on UCLA. We were in their faces while their backs were against the wall. We didn't want to force a game 3, so we had to jump out early and shut them up fast. It was a pitcher's duel between Michael Roth and Rob Rasmussen. UCLA took a 1-0 lead in the fifth inning, but when the bottom of the eighth approached, things started getting sweaty. Brady Thomas got things rolling with a leadoff single, and Robert Beary came in to pinch run for him. Kyle Enders then advanced Beary to second on a ground out. It was then up to me with one out and the tying run in scoring position. I went into a long at bat, taking balls and fouling off strikes. Then, the 2-2 pitch was delivered and I swung and chopped it to the left side of the first baseman. I smelled trouble and thought I might be out, but as the first baseman went to backhand it, the ball trickled off his glove and into right field – just past the out-stretched hand of the second baseman. THE GAME WAS TIED! The crowd was roaring my name so loud that I could barely hear myself think on first base. My dad, who could not sit in his seat, later told me he was standing in the center field bleachers while the fans were rocking with 'Haney', 'Haney', 'Haney'. It was an amazing moment – a turning point for USC.

We had plenty of chances to win game 2 before we went into extra innings, but couldn't capitalize. UCLA also had several chances but Matt Price shut them down. As soon as we went into extra innings, the tension built more and more. In the 11th inning, Wingo made it to third base with one out, and Whit Merrifield stepped to the plate, the tension eased a little bit more because we knew the trophy was ours. Sure enough, Whit hit a shot down the first base line that drove in the winning run, and we won game 2 of the CWS, 2-1. *College Baseball history!*

When we won the CWS, we dog piled on top of Whit. I made sure I was on top since I almost suffocated on the bottom of the pile during the win in the Super Regionals. After we got up and were congratulating each other, Coach Tanner said to me, "Can you believe we won the National Championship with you at shortstop?" We both laughed and hugged one another. It was one of greatest feelings of my life. It almost didn't seem real because this is the kind of stuff you dream about.

There is no better feeling in the world than winning the whole thing. As a little kid, no matter what league you are in or how old you are, winning is an extraordinary accomplishment. The best part about winning a championship is that all the fans love you and they are winners too! Looking back on the National Championship, it's hard to comprehend. You start to think how it happened and why it happened a certain way. When you win you have to have so many things go right for you and your teammates. I hate to admit it, but the South Carolina baseball team in 2010 was not only talented, we were lucky as well. You go over every little thing you did and think about how it helped win the title. I had a string of things running through my head, "If I hadn't made that play or got that hit or made an error or didn't take that pitch, what would have happened? What if our starting pitchers had gotten hurt or what if we played nervous and uptight throughout the World Series?" All these little factors come into play and had an impact on us winning the championship.

When you set out to start a season in any sport, your main goal is to win the whole thing, but the chances of you winning the whole thing are slim to none. There are hundreds of other teams who compete for the same thing you do, so the odds of making it to Omaha to compete aren't too high. We wanted to win the championship because of all the hard work we put in through the year, and we felt like we deserved it. We talked about going to the World Series and winning it, but we had to do it and not just talk about it. You can't just coast to the CWS—you have to prepare and work hard. We practiced and lifted weights and studied hard all year long so we could have a good chance to go to Omaha and win it all. One of the best things that the South Carolina baseball team did to win the National Championship was focus and maintain our composure. No matter what happened to us, we never lost our focus or let losses get to us mentally throughout the season. That carried us into the National Championship. If someone struck out, we wouldn't beat ourselves up. If someone made an error, then we had to get the next play. We had to put the negative things behind us and move on to the next play. It is hard to do that after you mess up, but our team morale was at the highest level. If you messed up, the other guys on the team would tell you that it would be okay. We were very supportive of each other and surrounded ourselves with positive thinking.

When you win a National Championship for a major city and for a bunch of dedicated fans, you feel like you're in a fairy tale and that nothing can go wrong. When we won I hugged my father and I started to tear up because it was so surreal. I pointed up to the sky and thanked God for letting us be on this earth and play this fantastic game and come out on top. There are many reasons why people want to become National Champions and we knew the right reasons in our hearts. It wasn't so we could be on television or to get more meal money and batting gloves. We wanted to be National Champions because we wanted to have that label on us that we are the best. We wanted to win a National Championship for our school, our city, our state, our team and most importantly, for our passionate fans. So many Gamecock fans waited their entire lives for the baseball team to win a National Championship, and we knew we had to bring it to them. Our baseball team made history by winning the CWS, and not only was it the first National Championship for the baseball team, it was the first national title for one of the major athletic programs at USC as well.

Gamecock fans always make me laugh because they always come up and say to me, "Hey Bobby, thank you for everything man, you guys played great." I tell them thanks right back. Without our fans and support it would have been hard to win it all. We had desire and strong motivation to win the World Series for the fans of Gamecock Nation. When the team and I were at autograph signings, the fans would come through the line and always talk about how they wanted us to take another trip back to Omaha. Some of them would talk about winning it all, but all of them talked about going to Omaha. Our fans were just not going to settle for anything less than Omaha anymore.

After we won the National Championship, the team was almost speechless. When we got back from Rosenblatt and back to the hotel, I couldn't believe how many people were in the lobby of our hotel. Every single Gamecock fan that went to the World Series in the past week was there waiting on us. The hotel looked like a circus as we were greeted with so much love and respect. Everyone was hugging and kissing us and asking for autographs. Even though we were mentally exhausted from celebrating and crying on the field, we were still hyper and excited for the fans waiting for us. We had just won the College World Series in the final year of Rosenblatt Stadium! I wanted to soak the moment in for as long as I could. I don't think any of us went to bed that night!

When we left for Carolina in the morning, we were truly exhausted and were not looking forward to the plane ride back, but we were pumped up to bring the trophy back home to South Carolina where it belonged. When we got off the plane and got on the bus, we headed to the Colonial Life Arena where our basketball team plays. The arena was not being used for basketball on this day, however. When we pulled up to the arena, there was a camera guy filming us coming off the bus with the trophy. We knew some of our fans were inside patiently waiting for us to arrive. When we walked into the arena, we were standing behind a curtain waiting to enter the court. While we waited, we could hear the fans chanting and our walkout song 2001 was blasting. The exhausted feeling soon went away and we couldn't wait to see all the fans waiting for us in the arena. As soon as they lifted the curtain, the fans started to go nuts and cheer at the top of their lungs. To our amazement there were probably 15 to 20,000 people there. It was crazy! We made our lap around the arena as all the fans pointed and cheered our names looking down at us. It was one of the most memorable feelings I have ever had. My team and I were a part of something great and historic. The fans were so proud of all of us, and we were thankful for that.

When we entered the arena, team captains Kyle Enders and Jay Brown held the trophy up high above their shoulders. We finally brought the trophy home to Columbia. I never wanted that day to end because I felt so proud of my teammates and myself. I wanted to walk around that basketball court all day long and have the crowd going nuts. After things calmed down a little, we were introduced on stage, one by one. When Coach Tanner got on stage with the National Championship trophy in his hands, he raised the trophy up above his head and screamed, "How about that, Gamecock Nation!" I was stunned because I never saw Coach Tanner this excited before. Nothing could make us unhappy on this day, nothing. Then, Whit Merrifield, Jackie Bradley Jr. and Blake Cooper said a few gracious words and thanked Gamecock Nation from the bottom of their hearts. Next, Scott Wingo took the mike and shouted our pre-game ritual of "I bet you won't get crunk!" The fans loved it. When I left the basketball arena with my team, I didn't know if I would ever have that feeling again, but it turns out I did.

A couple of nights later, a couple of guys on the team and I hit up downtown because we were all 21 years of age or older. We went from place to place, but spent most of the time at this one joint. That night everyone knew who we were when we walked in and we had plenty to eat and drink. The night got so crazy with celebration that by 1 am, my buddy Nick Ebert and I were taking over the place. The owner was cool and we had a great time with our fans!

The next day was the National Championship parade and Ebert and I got up so late that we almost missed it. We took a bus to the heart of the city in Columbia and each of us got on a float with a couple of other players. My float was the best because the SC cheerleaders were on it and we had the National Championship trophy. Rolling through the city, you could see people lining the streets everywhere you looked. People were yelling, cheering and pointing at us on the floats like we were the New York Yankees or something. The fans were holding up signs and taking all the pictures they could. I honestly did feel like a Yankee as I had a cigar in my mouth, pointing and smiling as I was holding up the National Trophy. People were shouting out of their office building windows way up on the 20th floor. We all loved every minute of it!

Our floats then stopped at the State House where the mayor stood waiting for us. We got up on the steps in front of the State House where the Gamecock flag was proudly raised for all in the city of Columbia to see. The fans went crazy and cheered, as it was truly a proud moment in Gamecock history. When the mayor took the stage, he had a Gamecock hat on and had the greatest things to say about our team and our lovely city. He presented Coach Tanner and the team with a key to the city. The Mayor stated at the end of his speech that from now on, July 1st is going to be known as Gamecock National Champions Day. We had a day to ourselves named after us and everything—it was unbelievable!

◆ CHAPTER NINE ◆

I'm Not in College Anymore

I knew when I turned down the opportunity to play professional baseball that I might never get another chance like that again. That's a risk baseball players take when they turn down money or turn down the draft. I figured when I turned down the draft out of high school that I would become a better player and person. Junior year at South Carolina was supposed to be my year since I didn't get signed out of junior college, which made me mad. During my junior year, I got off to a slow start and wasn't drafted. I was not truly upset about it, since I knew the surgery I had on my shoulder would likely keep me from being drafted. When senior year at South Carolina rolled around, I knew that I had no more baseball eligibility left. It was either get drafted or try to sign with a major league team somewhere on my own. At the end of my junior season, Coach Tanner told me in his office that the scouts thought I would be an excellent senior sign, whatever that meant. I wanted very badly to get drafted my senior year because I wanted to play professional baseball more than anything.

Scouts would always come to South Carolina to check out our players and see who was performing well. There was always a tremendous amount of exposure at USC because we play in the best conference in the country, the SEC. I had to fill out a bunch of questionnaires from all different major league ball clubs, just like some of the other guys on the team did. I would get excited, but would then forget about it because I knew nothing was guaranteed.

I started to receive phone calls from different pro scouts in early May 2010 about signing. The scouts would ask me how badly I wanted to play professional baseball and wanted to know if I was serious or if I wanted to play just to say I played pro ball. I told them I wanted to play more than anything in the world and that I would sign for anything. I knew I was not going to get any money because I was a senior. A senior does not really have a choice, which is why big league clubs sign seniors out of college for little or no bonus money.

When the beginning of June rolled around, there were only a couple of scouts calling me and I was still not positive I was going to be drafted. You never know if you are going to be drafted until draft day rolls around and your name is called. The teams that I thought were seriously interested in me at the time were the Kansas City Royals, the Cincinnati Reds and the Toronto Blue Jays. I didn't care which team drafted me as long as I was selected by one of them. A couple of days before the draft, I looked on the updated draft tracker and didn't like what I saw. I didn't see my name, but I saw a bunch of guys on my team listed. I knew that the draft tracker was not a big deal, but I was mad and very frustrated that my name was not on there at all.

Day 1 of the draft went by slow since they only called the first round, and my name wasn't called, but I didn't really expect it to be called, anyway. The second day of the draft was very exciting for our whole team, since we had a couple of our guys get selected that day. In the fourth round, the Blue Jays selected our fireball pitcher Sam Dyson. At this time, we were about to begin practice at Carolina Stadium and get ready for the Super Regionals. We couldn't start practice until our right fielder, Whit Merrifield, was drafted. Whit waited in the training room and watched the draft as we all waited for him outside on the field. When Whit finally came out onto the field, we had already heard the news. Whit was selected in the 9th round by the Kansas City Royals. A couple of rounds later in the 12th round, the Arizona Diamond Backs selected our ace Blake Cooper. Coop was excited more than anything because it was his first time getting drafted. As practice came to an end, I went home with a massive headache due to the sun and the heat.

When I got home, I sat on the couch with Danielle and listened to the draft over the Internet. I started watching and listening to the draft in the 15th round. I was dozing off because I was not feeling too good, but I was trying to stay awake because I knew that there was a chance my name might be called. When the 21st round was coming to an end, I was feeling negative and didn't think I was going to get picked up at all. My girlfriend suggested that maybe I would be drafted in the 23rd round since that was my jersey number. I didn't care which round I was picked in, as long as I was drafted.

When the 22nd round arrived, Danielle and I were quiet and we listened intently as the SF Giants started to select a player. Then we heard...

"*The San Francisco Giants select...Haney, Robert, a shortstop from the University of South Carolina-Columbia.*"

We looked at each other and started cheering like crazy. I gave Danielle a hug and then she started to cry her eyes out because she was so excited for me. The headache I had was slowly going away.

A couple of minutes later, the calls and text messages started to flood my cell phone. The first call this time was from my mother. She was so thrilled for me and was wondering why the Giants drafted me, since they never talked to me before the draft. When my scout Jeremy Cleveland called to congratulate me, he asked if I remembered him. I didn't have much of a response, but said, "Yeah, I think so." He told me that he was there at the beginning of the season, and he and another scouting director for the Giants liked everything about me. They selected me mainly because of how I play on defense, since I did not really swing the bat that well until the end of the season. I didn't care because I knew that I was finally selected and the San Francisco Giants were my new family.

After we won the College World Series, I was exhausted, but I had to sign as soon as possible and then head to Arizona for the summer for rookie ball. Guys who get drafted or sign late into the summer are usually sent to rookie ball. It was a change from the luxury I had back at South Carolina. We didn't get handed everything and we were not treated like kings at all. Once you are in the minor leagues, no matter how high of a draft pick you are, no one really cares who you are. You are just one of the many players in the minor leagues trying to make it to the majors. My first practice was a little rough because I had trouble getting used to the 112-degree heat, even though it was dry. I did make some mistakes by trying way too hard to make spectacular plays. The next day, when I came into the locker room for practice, I went over to my locker and it was gone! Some of the pitchers wheeled my locker into the bathroom facing the urinal. All of my equipment was completely taped up, including my wristbands and on the tape, it said "Johnny McFlare Flare." It was an amusing prank and I couldn't get mad and cry about it, so I had to just roll with it. It was extremely embarrassing to unwrap all my stuff and wheel my locker back into its place, but it's all part of being the new guy, I guess.

From there on out, things got much better, and I got used to the Arizona heat. The first professional game I played in I went 1 for 4 with an RBI. My first base hit was a rocket over the second baseman's head into the gap. It felt good to get on the board in the first game with a rope of a base hit. During the season, I struggled like everyone else does in baseball and our hitting coach created a new stance for me so that I could hit more line drives and get to the hitting zone much quicker. I was hitting .300 at the beginning of my season and then dipped all the way below .200. I broke out of my 0 for 14 slump and finished hitting around .240, which was not terrible, but not great either. When my parents came to visit me in Arizona, I had one of the worst games of my career. I went 0 for 5 with an error at shortstop. I was so mad after the game I barely spoke to my parents at dinner that night. That was wrong of me to act like that because games like that happen. I hit so many balls hard that summer, but right at people. My swing was better than my college swing and I was happy about that.

Some people don't have a clue how professional baseball players are treated and how they live in the minor leagues. People think we get to eat the best food, get paid a lot of money and stay in the nicest hotels. When I asked for a pair of batting gloves on my first day at the ballpark, the equipment manager said, "Okay, that will be 25 bucks." I almost didn't believe it, but I paid him the money because at the time I had no batting gloves whatsoever. At South Carolina, we got a pair of gloves whenever we needed them.

During my first year of pro ball in Arizona, I stayed in the Days Inn Hotel for $7 a night, which came out of my monthly paycheck. That was reasonable considering some guys had $22 per night taken out of their paychecks for staying at the Hilton. We basically lived out of our suitcases and had no transportation. Some guys get paid as low as $280 every two weeks. I got paid about $380 every two weeks. It's not much, but you are still getting a paycheck to play the game of baseball, which is awesome. Our away games are only about an hour away at most, but sometimes our air conditioning wouldn't work well, so we would have to sweat for a little bit before we got to the field. No one ever said it was going to be easy in the minor leagues—it's a grind, for sure. You start out in Arizona at the beginning of March and play about 130 games into September. The minor leagues are not for everyone, which is why some guys quit after their first or second year. If you love the game of baseball like I do, then you will have no problem getting through the minor league grind. My life is between the lines on the diamond, and I like it that way. Most of the days I would walk into the locker room wearing my South Carolina shirts and shorts because it was hot out, and that's all I had to wear at that time. All my buddies would say, "Wow, close your yearbook Haney, seriously." This meant they wanted me to stop living in the past. It was hard for me to close my yearbook since we had just won the National Championship, and I was proud. At this level, though, it didn't matter what you did in college because this was the big time. You had a clean slate and a wood bat in your hand from here on out.

I was put on the cover of Baseball Express® and on the inside cover of Baseball America® Magazine during my first year of pro ball. I couldn't believe they picked me to be on the cover. The pictures were of me fielding and hitting, with Blake Cooper in the middle, pitching. It was a shock to be on the cover of a magazine. I used to order out of that magazine when I was a little boy. The National Championship at South Carolina ended up being bigger for me than I had thought.

After the 2010 college baseball season and rookie ball came to an end, I was looking forward to kicking up my feet in South Carolina and relaxing. I was ready to attend the football games and tailgate with my boys. While in South Carolina, I took classes at USC during the fall semester. I thought all the traveling was going to be put to a stop for a while, but I was wrong. The Gamecocks were invited up to Washington D.C. to meet the President of the United States, Barack Obama, for winning a National Championship.

The Gamecocks and about 30 other National Championship teams from around the country were all invited. I thought that this event was a once in a lifetime opportunity, so I was not going to miss this roadtrip! On the first day we were there, we took a tour of the Washington Nationals ballpark, went inside the locker room and got to go on the field, which was refreshing. Later on that day, we were taken on a tour of Congress and then headed to the White House. We waited on the White House lawn for President Obama to come out from his office, and after a couple of hours he emerged, and walked up to the podium. He gave a short speech that inspired all the athletes and he told us he was proud and honored to be with us. He then went around and shook our hands. When he got to me, I froze up. President Obama asked, "Are you on the baseball team as well?" I replied, "Yes, appreciate it." I couldn't believe I really said that, but I didn't care too much because I had just shaken the president's hand, and that's all that mattered. *It was thrilling!*

✦ EPILOGUE ✦

I have now finished two seasons in the minor leagues and plan to stick with it and try to make it to the majors. Every day on the diamond is a learning experience, and I plan to keep soaking in as much as I can. Playing in the minor leagues has prepared me for life, and I have developed into a stronger player, not only physically, but mentally as well. It isn't going to be easy to make it to the major leagues, but nothing worth doing in life comes easy.

Later on in life I plan to become the head coach of a division I baseball team. I have seen many good examples of coaching from my playing days – from my first coach, my Dad, to Coach Musmacker and onward to Coach Tanner, and I believe I can be a successful coach and produce a championship team one day.

With everything that I have learned in my baseball career, I would like to pass my experiences on down to younger players, in hopes that they too might get a championship ring of their own.

◆ Why I Wrote This Book ◆

The main reason that I wrote this book was because I wanted people to know about my baseball and school experiences. I wanted young players and parents to know about my successes and failures as a baseball player.

Many kids all over the world have dreams of winning the College World Series and becoming a professional baseball player. There are always ups and downs. I thought that by writing my story it would give kids the inspiration to succeed in sports and in life.

– Bobby Haney

✦ ACKNOWLEDGEMENTS ✦

I want to first and foremost thank my family for helping me on my journey: Mom, Dad, and my Brothers Brian & Brandon.

Special thanks to my Grandparents for their love and never ending support: Grandma JoAnn, Grandpa Bob, Grandma Haney, Grandpa Haney and Patti.

Special thanks to all my Aunts, Uncles and Cousins, especially Uncle Rob, Aunt Mary Ellen, Uncle Tuite, Aunt Ann Marie, Uncle Kevin, Uncle Rick, Aunt Debbie, Uncle Scot & Paul. Cousins: Christopher, Justin, Josh, Sammi, Rebecca, Jonathan & Caela, Gail & Ron, Joey, Curtis & Michael, Nancy & Paul, Kurt, Nancy & Ed, Billy & Eileen, Patrick, Michael & Ann, Harry & Max, Andrea & Bruce, Lewis & Julia, Vicki & Nicole, Vicki, Stephen & Laura, Richard & Victoria, Great Aunt Rose, Great Uncle Dickie, Great Aunt Stella, Great Aunt Joanie, Great Uncle Frank & Judy, Great Uncle Donnie, Great Aunt Linda, Great Aunt Rita. Great, Great Aunt Angie, Great, Great Aunt Louise, The Caswells, The Pearces, The Sadoskys, The Panas & Roach family, Tedescos and Viccoras, The Zilbermans, The Talbots & Donna Losty, all the Cases, New Jersey Haneys and Gambardellas near and far!

My continued thanks for always supporting me:
The Habers, The Reichmans, The O'Connors, The Negris, The Ryans, The Ragostas, The Serraltas, The Tjadens, and The Mundinger Families.

Thanks to all my Coaches, Advisors, Trainers & Doctors:
Bob Wilborg, Bob Hoffman, John Dekams, Wayne Miron, Mark Goldstein, Bob Brown, Kevin Chirameda, Rick Riccobono, Al Chandler, Mike Prisco, Duke Durland, Ed Duddy, Don & Sue Whiston, Mike Sabino, Bill LaMura, Tony Annunziata, Jim Clark, Eric Joyner, Ray Babinski, Lou Petrucci, Mike Quigley, Ken Ferrazzi, John Furia, Ray Tanner, Tim Hill, Tim Hill II, Al Corbeil, Barry Batson, Mark Calvi, Sammy Esposito, Chad Holbrook, Monte Lee, Steven Bondurant, Matt Ennis, Brainard Cooper, Kelly Aherns, Neil Somers, Paul Gibson, Mike Kain, Dr. Mary DeRose, John Musmacker, Pete Blieberg, Pat Short, Sal Puccio, Larry Izzo, Dr. David Dines, Dr. Harold Van Bosse, Dr. Chris Mazoue, Brian Newberry and Chuck Alben. Thanks also to Smithtown Recreation for some great Summers!

Thanks to all my extended baseball families and friends for your support and kind wishes over the years:
The Sweeneys (Bill, my statistician), Sabellas, Belfiores, Mangiones, Dekams, Melansons, Locrotondos, Browns, Mirons, Romanos, Kumps, Smiths, Sommos, Bairds, Loparos, DeVannas, Wilborgs, Konfinos, McGees, Ryans, Matt Harris & Family, Steve & Robert Clark, Kalousdians, Garrets, Rockhills, Waschenkos Tuortos, Hammonds, Lunds, Kazemis, Vetranos, Ferris, Sykes, Petruccis, Ripps

Pearses, Laudadios, Goldsteins, Agueces, Holmes, Garcias, Sannas, Foleys, Hochmans, Cassettas, Damicos, Liangs, Shipkoskis, Paces, Messinas, Castellos, Harris, Goings, Tullys, Gallos, Stupnikovs, Jonkes, Brigandis, Aherns, Guercios, Fitzpatricks, Gallos, Tekverks, Rossis, Gregorys, Dorseys, Wiltons, Albaneses, Liparis, Gormans, Friedmans, Raffertys, Shearmans, Alfieris, Skurnicks, Phillips, Quigleys, Lukasiewics, Piazzas, Zarembas, Smyths, Pappishs, Weisbaums, Wolffs, Panettieris, Scherbs, Dennehys, Lynns, Bartleys, Scanlons, Muratores, Dichiaras, Lopiperos, Steidls, D'angelos, Galanoudis, Bushmans, McLeods, Mulls, Wedlers, Blooms, Bennets, Dohertys, Andy Gregory (my Manatee photographer), Eric Citron, Jack Cust & Diamond Nation, Dave Pfeiffer, Greg Sarra, Austin Yeager & BT, Aberles, John Brooks, John Valenzuela, Kerstetters, Geremias, Mike Fitzpatrick, Luzims, Stephans, Neil Heaton, Dave Barnett, Skellys, McCarthys, Gracis, Kellys, McDermotts, Owsinskis, O'Learys, Mangognas, Murphys, Persichillis, Silvas, Sherrows, Brechisis, Goodmans, Tius, Lanieris, Scavuzzos, Chicoskys, Buckleys, Brian Glen, Grandma's OTB friends, Mom's friends at the Kings Park School District, KP Buildings & Grounds, Campisis, Bishops, Bryan & Jimmy Goelz, Joe Francisco, Matt Guiliano, Evan Deitch, Bob Kenney, Ciliottas, Kizis, Terrells, Arenas, Coronas, Tursis, Brian Bechtel, Fred Maiorino & Family, Reeds, Oddos, Bermans, CHSS Family, Mr. B, Coach O'Brien, Johnstons, Yackels, McGinleys, Chris Ferry & Family, Langrocks, DeMotts, Ann Rogers, Kuhrts, Restivos, Paguagas, Thornhills, Corazzatas, The Long Island Tigers, The Long Island Titans, The Long Island Bulls, St. Joseph's Church & CYO, Kings Park Youth, Leo Ostebo, Wanda Zimmerman, Kristi Davis and all my South Carolina families & friends.

Special thanks to all my professors and teachers - I appreciate all that you have done for me. Thanks for putting up with me!

Thanks to Kyle Lipsey for designing the South Carolina 2010 National Championship ring.

What can I say? Thank you to my Personal Coach and Advisor, Gil Matos and his great family, Wanda, Justin, Gil and Brandon.

My Sincere thanks to the scouts that drafted me: Sal Agostinelli of the Phillies and Jeremy Cleveland of the Giants.

Many thanks to all my teammates over the years - we had a lot of fun!

Special thanks to Tom Locrotondo and Tim Melanson for always making sure our Kings Park ball fields were in top playing condition.

In Remembrance:
Great Grandma Stella, Great Grandma Tootsie, Great Grandma Case, Great Grandma Haney, Great Grandma Tjaden, Great Uncle Jack Haney, Great Uncle Angelo, and Bayler Teal. To my Great Uncle Vic Viccora – sorry I missed you - Manatee was fun, I know that you were somewhere in the stands!